Hull
TROLLEYBUSES

Paul Morfitt and Malcolm Wells

Series editor Robert J Harley

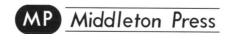

MP Middleton Press

Cover picture: Few trolleybuses could be considered as being before their time but the "Coronations" could be so described. In this photograph no. 102 displays the Roe body to perfection as it rests at the Endike Lane terminus. Note the red triangle in the centre lower deck window which was carried by all trolleybuses on both sides and in the rear downstairs window to inform other drivers that the vehicle was a trolleybus. The view is a summer one, as the crew member is wearing the lightweight jacket issued to staff for that season. (Authors' collections)

First Published February 2004

ISBN 1 904474 24 1

© *Middleton Press, 2004*

Design   *Deborah Esher*
                   David Pede

Published by
                   Middleton Press
                   Easebourne Lane
                   Midhurst, West Sussex
                   GU29 9AZ
Tel: 01730 813169
Fax: 01730 812601
Email: info@middletonpress.co.uk
www.middletonpress.co.uk

Printed & bound by MPG Books, Bodmin, Cornwall

CONTENTS

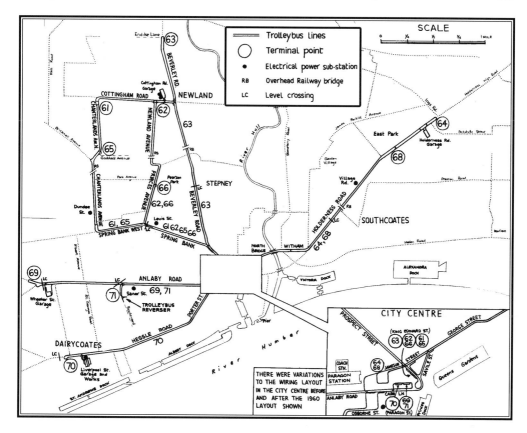

INTRODUCTION AND ACKNOWLEDGEMENTS

The two authors first met after the publication of Malcolm's history of the system in 1997. They share an equal enthusiasm for Hull's trolleybuses and have gathered a wide range of information and photographs about the system, from which they have drawn the contents of this book. Compiling the information and selecting the photographs has been a labour of love for both authors.

Paul Morfitt was born six years after the last trolleybus ran. His interest in Hull's trolleybuses dates from a school project about local transport. In May 1988, after leaving school, he joined East Yorkshire Motor Services as a conductor when they were re-introduced to work on Routemasters. He obtained his PSV licence at the age of eighteen and moved to Kingston upon Hull City Transport as a driver where his duties involved working from the former trolleybus garage at Cottingham Road, but soon transferred to the Engineer's Department. He subsequently moved to Stagecoach in Hull.

His interest in the former Transport Undertaking has continued to grow and he has amassed some 5000 prints as well as many items and records connected with its history. Paul was fortunate to discover the Grant farebox that was fitted to "Coronation" no. 116 in 1956, hidden away in Liverpool Street Works. When wired up, it worked perfectly despite not having been used for over forty years.

For Malcolm Wells it seems like only yesterday that he travelled every day to and from school by trolleybus. This was the start of a continuing love affair with Hull's azure blue and white trolleybuses which has resulted in this book, a previous book and several published articles.

He visited relatives in Newland Avenue, went to school football and cricket matches, the cinema and city centre shops and, eventually, to work by trolleybus. He was present when abandonment began on 28th January 1961 and rode on no. 101 on its last journey to Cottingham Road Garage on 31st October 1964.

For a short time in 1964/65, he worked in the Works Section of KHCT, before moving elsewhere within local government, there being few prospects within the department at that time.

Wherever possible, the original photographer has been credited with the print, but several prints do not bear any indication of their origin or even a date. Should any photographers recognise their work, we hope that they will understand any lack of recognition. Many photographs were taken by the late Geoff O'Connell (Traffic Officer) and the late Les Storry (Foreman at Cottingham Road Garage) but the negatives were sold to well-known national providers and some that appear here under various names are the result of their enthusiasm and efforts. Only a small number of photographs have appeared in print before.

September 2003

Paul Morfitt
Malcolm J Wells

GEOGRAPHICAL SETTING

The city of Kingston upon Hull is located on the north bank of the River Humber, some fifty-five miles east of Leeds. The city itself is bisected by the River Hull. There are no hills or gradients of any note and the flat, straight main roads permitted trolleybuses to display their fast acceleration. For most of the trolleybus era, Hull's population was just under 300,000.

All the main roads were crossed on the level by at least one railway crossing. A 1954 census revealed that the Dairycoates crossing was closed to road traffic on 130 occasions for a total of six hours and twenty-four minutes per day between 7.00am and 11.00pm. All of which made timekeeping impossible at certain times.

In addition, the Holderness Road route crossed the River Hull by way of North Bridge, which was a Schweitzer rolling lift type bridge.

HISTORICAL BACKGROUND

Kingston upon Hull received its city charter from King Edward 1 in 1399, after which the city prospered. In 1774-78 its first dock was constructed and two more followed by 1830. By 1914 a further seven docks had been opened.

As the city grew in size a system of privately-operated horse trams on five routes had been constructed by 1877. A steam tramway to Marfleet followed in 1889. All these routes suffered from intense competition from wagonnettes and financial problems were experienced culminating in a municipal takeover. Conversion to electric operation commenced in July 1899 and was completed in 1900, when eight short routes were in operation. Between that date and 1927, the tramway system was extended several times to reach a maximum of 20.48 route miles employing 180 tramcars.

By 1927 a small network of motorbus services had been built up and it was the success of the Preston Road route that led to proposals for trolleybuses on a large scale.

Not until November 1934 were trolleybuses considered once more. By which time the outer portions of some tram routes had been replaced by motorbuses as part of a co-ordination agreement with East Yorkshire Motor Services limited. This divided the city into an inner area (the "A" area) wherein the corporation retained all the fares income and another area (the "B" area) where receipts and mileage were shared out on an annual basis. The remaining tram routes were all confined to the "A" area.

On the recommendation of the Acting General Manager, Mr J. Lawson, powers for the abandonment of the trams and operation of trolleybuses were obtained during 1936 and twenty-six trolleybuses were ordered for the initial conversions.

The system was officially inaugurated on 23rd July 1937, although the public service on services 61 and 61A to Chanterlands Avenue did not begin until 27th July. In October services 62 and 62A to Newland Avenue commenced operation. Both services were worked by twenty-six Leyland TB4 trolleybuses with Weymann H54R bodies. These were painted in the new streamlined azure blue and white livery and were equipped with unusual white destination blinds which used black lettering and numbers.

Twenty Crossley TDD4 trolleybuses with Cravens H54R bodies followed in 1938 and took over the Beverley Road route in September 1938.

All three routes were worked from Cottingham Road Garage and the two batches were physically separated within the garage and were employed only on their designated route. This lasted until wartime conditions dictated more intensive use of vehicles.

Another twenty trolleybuses were delivered to Cottingham Road in the Summer of 1939. These were Leyland TB7s with East Lancashire H54R bodies and were intended to open the Holderness Road route in September 1939. However, the outbreak of war in that month led to the opening being postponed. Four of the batch were licensed for use from Cottingham Road, but the remainder stayed in store until February 1940 when services 64 and 64A were introduced. All twenty vehicles were transferred to Holderness Road Garage for the service. Within a few weeks the route was extended across the city centre to a new terminus near the railway station.

Throughout 1941 and 1942 Hull was subjected to major bombing raids, which destroyed entirely the overhead within the city centre and a quarter of a mile radius from it. No trolleybuses were lost, but a direct hit on the central bus garage destroyed and damaged several motorbuses.

A most dramatic development was the painting out of all white areas of the livery using blue paint so that vehicles could not be seen from the air, particularly as most were now parked along main roads and in parks at night.

Another change was the replacement of the white blinds with black blinds carrying a single large service number to assist passengers in the blackout at night. Rear blinds were set to the white area to assist drivers with identifying vehicles in front of them in the blackout. Several pre-war blinds and large number blinds survived until the late fifties.

An additional trolleybus service was started in November 1941. Numbered 67, this ran from King Edward Street to Chanterlands Avenue North using the service 63 overhead on Beverley Road as far as Cottingham Road and the overhead along Cottingham Road past the garage to Chanterlands Avenue. This latter wiring was normally used only for garage workings. Service 67 ran every twenty minutes and was withdrawn on at least one occasion, but also ran later during the war and until 1949.

Four Leyland TB4s (nos 1-4) were loaned to Pontypridd for a time in 1942, but these were recalled in time to join nos 5-10 to replace trams on the Anlaby Road route, using materials salvaged from the routes abandoned in 1934.

This left only one tram route at work and this, the Hessle Road route, was replaced with trolleybuses on 1st July 1945. Twelve Sunbeam Ws with Brush bodies numbered 67 - 78 were delivered for this which brought the system up to a route mileage of 17.12 miles. These were delivered in an allover azure blue livery.

Repainting of the fleet into a revised version of the streamlined livery commenced in June 1945, Leyland no. 22 being the first to be so treated.

The hard pressed fleet was reinforced by six more Sunbeams with Roe bodies (nos 79-84) in late 1945. Paint supplies being still restricted these carried an allover royal blue livery. Not until the Spring of 1947 did six more Sunbeam Ws arrive. These were numbered 85 - 90 and carried the new standard large route number box and separate via box.

On 30th March 1947 the Anlaby Road route was extended a short distance from the roundabout at the Anlaby Road/Boothferry Road junction to Meadowbank Road.

Ten Sunbeam F4s with Roe eight feet wide bodies (nos 91-100) were delivered in May 1948 and they took over service 69 on 1st June leading to a round of reallocation of vehicles.

The fleet now reached its maximum of one hundred vehicles working six trolleybus routes all possessing a high frequency; the busiest being service 70 which required eighteen trolleybuses to maintain a peak two minute headway. The routes, together with their peak frequencies in brackets, were:-

61 King Edward Street - Spring Bank - Spring Bank West - Chanterlands Avenue North (4)
62 King Edward Street - Spring Bank - Princes Avenue-Newland Avenue (3/4)
63 King Edward Street - Beverley Road (Endike Lane) (2/3)
64 Jameson Street - George Street - Witham - Holderness Road (Ings Road) (2/3)
65 King Edward Street - Spring Bank - Spring Bank West - Chanterlands Avenue - Goddard Avenue
66 King Edward Street - Spring Bank - Princes Avenue-Pearson Park
68 Jameson Street - George Street - Witham - Holderness Road (East Park)
69 Waterworks Street - Anlaby Road - Meadowbank Road (2/3)
70 Waterworks Street - Osborne Street - Porter Street - Hessle Road - Dairycoates (2)
71 Waterworks Street - Anlaby Road - Boulevard.

Services 65/66/68/71 were short workings of services 61/62/64/69. Waterworks Street became part of Paragon Street in 1952.

To meet the heavy post-war traffic demands all trolleybuses numbered between 1 and 84 were reseated, the TB4s to fifty-six, the Crossleys and TB7s first to fifty-six and then to sixty. Nos 67 to 84 were also increased to sixty seats.

The hub of the system was Queen Victoria Square in which, until March 1959 when services 64/68 were re-routed, all six routes could be observed. In 1948 no fewer than one hundred and thirty-five journeys were scheduled to pass through the square at peak times.

By 1950 the oldest trolleybuses were thirteen years old and thoughts turned to replacement vehicles. Mr Pulfrey, the General Manager, had visited the United States and Europe and had become convinced that one man operation was the way forward.

Accordingly, in conjunction with the Sunbeam Trolleybus Company Limited and Charles H Roe, a new design of trolleybus was produced that was suitable for operation by the driver only. This trolleybus, numbered 101 was constructed in 1952 and was exhibited at the Commercial Motor Show at Earl's Court. It carried a fifty-four seat dual doorway body and was equipped with Earl trolley retrievers and a periscope to enable drivers to see how many passengers occupied the top deck.

Not until January 1953 did it enter service in Hull where, as 1953 was coronation year, crews gave it the "Coronation" nickname, a description which was also applied to the production batch.

No. 101 was operated on each service in number order for a period of six weeks but its stay on service 70 was cut short as it could not cope with the intense traffic on Hessle Road. After this no.101 was allocated to Cottingham Road Garage. Fifteen further "Coronations" entered service in 1954 and 1955 and took over exclusive operation of service 63 from 1st May 1955. By which time all the Leyland TB4s had been withdrawn together with Crossley no. 46 whose lower deck was donated to a children's playground.

The fleet now stood at eighty-nine trolleybuses of which eighty-six were in service on Saturdays and seventy-six in the weekday peak. No works specials were operated but additional trolleybuses were provided for Hull City AFC matches at Boothferry Park situated near the service 69 terminus, Hull RFLC matches at the Boulevard for which a reverser was provide at Malm Street and Hull Kingston Rovers whose Craven Park ground adjoined the Holderness Road Garage.

Special workings were also provided for the annual week long Hull Fair in October. Extras on service 61 used a turning circle at Chanterlands Avenue South but those on service 69 worked though to each terminus. On Whit Sunday the Sailors' Orphans Homes held an annual gala which saw crowds of over 20,000 attending travelling mostly by service 62. Trolleybuses were borrowed from other garages and it was not unknown for every available vehicle to be in service on a Saturday when Hull City had crowds of more than 30,000 spectators

From 29th July 1952 alternate journeys on the Holderness Road route were curtailed at East Park as service 68 in order to save 60,000 miles and £3,000 a year.

"Coronation" no. 116 was equipped with a Grant farebox imported from Canada and an electronic passenger counter in connection with discussions with the Ministry of Transport and Civil Aviation about one-man operation. The farebox worked well but the counter proved to be anything but consistent. In the event, despite considerable negotiations and correspondence, no authorisation was ever obtained from the ministry.

Service 61 was always the least used of the

trolleybus services and in 1957, for a time the off-peak service worked only to Goddard Avenue, a reversion to the situation on its introduction in 1937. After protests from passengers it reverted to the full route.

However, Mr Pulfrey was determined to reduce costs and, in December 1958, he obtained authority from the Transport Committee for the purchase of ten single deck Sunbeam trolleybuses to be fitted with Roe bodywork to a thirty-five feet length. These would be numbered 1 to 10. This time the Ministry of Transport and Civil Aviation proved more accommodating and, in March 1959, gave full permission for the operation of the vehicles on services 61/65 and for one-man operation.

Sadly, the order was never confirmed because the problem of falling traffic (down to 35 million in 1958 from 53 million in 1949) and the re-location of residents from inner city areas to new estates beyond the trolleybus termini caused a re-appraisal.

Neither management nor the Transport Committee were anti-trolleybus. Indeed, some committee members were actively promoting extensions, particularly to Preston Road. But, economic facts could not be ignored and, after a year-long debate in which the trolleybuses received a relatively fair hearing, the decision to abandon was confirmed by the City Council on 3rd January 1960. By this time frequency reductions had been matched by vehicle withdrawals (mostly TB7s) and the fleet had been reduced to seventy-five trolleybuses.

The original abandonment plan saw service 69 as the first casualty owing to a faulty sub-station near Saner Street. A new road bridge was planned for Dairycoates to eliminate the level crossing and, although plans for diverting the service 70 terminus had been agreed, it was decided to convert service 70 before work started and to close the operational part of the Liverpool Street site. Trolleybuses requiring attention at Liverpool Street would to be towed there and back.

For each conversion the vehicles to be withdrawn would be transferred to the garage concerned immediately preceding the event and, on the first Saturday of 1961, the remaining Leyland TB7s and a few Crossleys were sent to Liverpool Street. Saturday, 28th January was chosen as the final day which turned to be wet and cold. Leyland no. 48 worked the last scheduled journey at 11.00pm from Paragon Street but the final trolleybus was Crossley no. 29 which worked a dance special at 11.42pm.

Service 69 succumbed one year later on Saturday, 3rd February 1962. in the middle of January all the remaining Crossleys were allocated to Wheeler Street. The last trolleybus was no. 34 which left Paragon Street at 11.00pm.

The Chanterlands Avenue route was replaced on Saturday, 28th July 1962, "Coronation" no. 108 being the last trolleybus. This meant the end of the special workings for Hull Fair. Wiring from Chanterlands Avenue North to Cottingham Road was retained for a time for the testing of newly overhauled or serviced trolleybuses.

The transfer of the remaining Sunbeam Ws to Holderness Road in August 1963 heralded the end of services 64 and 68. This came on 21st September with the last duty performed by no. 90.

Enthusiasts expected that the Sunbeam F4s would last until late 1964 with the "Coronations" going in 1965. So it was with great surprise that they greeted the announcement that service 62 would be abandoned in November 1963. No. 94 worked the last journey on 16th November 1963.

All sixteen "Coronations" were retained for service 63. In June 1964 service 63 was re-routed as part of a one-way system via Paragon Street, Chapel Street and Jameson Street in the city centre. The new overhead did not last for very long for Saturday, 31st October 1964 was to be the last day. No official acknowledgement of the event was made although no. 101 performed the last journey with no. 116, working a duplicate running one minute in front. With little ceremony no. 101 entered Cottingham Road for the last time and the system died after running 55,839,135 miles and carrying 887,387,582 passengers.

Attempts by the Reading Transport Society (later the British Trolleybus Society) to preserve a "Coronation" were rejected by the Transport Committee and when Sunbeam W no.80 was discovered still in existence in a Bingley scrapyard in 1984, the museums service decided that it was too far gone to be a realistic proposition for preservation. Today, only a few traction poles remain to remind us of the trolleybuses but they are still remembered with affection by those of Hull's citizens fortunate enough to have ridden on them.

QUEEN VICTORIA SQUARE

1.   Queen Victoria Square was the hub of the system through which all six routes passed until March 1959, when services 64/68 were re-routed. A survey in 1957 revealed that a total of 8,853 journeys a week were made by trolleybuses, the highest being service 70 with 2,338 and the lowest being service 61 with 873. Leyland TB4 no. 25, in original streamlined livery, circles the statue and toilets in the centre of the square in order to reach the King Edward Street barrier. (Authors'collections)

2.   Another view of the square shows Leyland TB7 no. 65 emerging from Savile Street on service 64 and bound for Carr Lane. On the left can be seen the three sidings for the service 61/2/3 termini. The day is probably a Sunday, judging by the sparse number of pedestrians. (Authors'collections)

3.   The last day of service 70 was wet and cold, as can be seen in this picture of Leyland TB7 no. 54 which is passing the front of the City Hall before turning into Paragon Street towards the terminus. "Coronation" no. 111 is leading a Crossley around the Queen Victoria statue to reach the loading points in King Edward Street.
(R. F. Mack)

KING EDWARD STREET

4.   This view, taken in October 1941, shows King Edward Street with an unidentified Crossley at the service 61 terminus. Several new poles had to be erected to replace those destroyed and the rosettes that were attached to the sides of now demolished buildings. Because of the exposed location, and to assist with coping with large queues, long shelters, each bearing a large service number, were installed at each terminal point. These lasted until the mid-fifties.(KHCA)

5.   This photograph, taken on the same day, shows the devastation on the opposite side of King Edward Street that resulted from the heavy bombing raids of May/June 1941, when all the overhead in the city centre and that within a quarter mile radius was destroyed. All three northern area services (61/2/3) can be seen as well as the single siding that was provided for them at that time. Note the direction sign for an air raid shelter. Post-war development was slow and not until 1952 were new shops and offices constructed here.(KHCA)

6.   By the early fifties some Brush-bodied Sunbeam Ws had moved from Liverpool Street to Cottingham Road Garage including no. 73 which is approaching the service 63 barrier, possibly in Coronation Year (1953) as the Ferens Art Gallery is suitably decorated. No. 73 is in as-delivered condition, although it has been repainted into the streamlined livery with the early post-war lettering and fleet numbers. (R. F. Mack)

7.   On Sunday 1st November 1959 three "Coronations" were photographed at the termini of the three northern services. It was unusual for all three services to be worked by MF2Bs on a Sunday. Nos 113 and 114 are nearest the camera. As can be seen, no protection from the elements was provided for passengers at this time, the shelters provided during the war having been removed. (L. R. Storry)

8.   This is the same location on what is obviously a quiet night. No. 105 is already standing at the service 63 barrier, whilst the conductor of no. 111 is holding down the "trigger" to allow it to enter the siding. (R.F.Mack)

9.   Just before 11pm on Saturday 28th July 1962, "Coronation" no. 105 stands at the service barrier ready to work the final service 61 journey. Motorman Jim Marshall is poised to take no. 105 to Chanterlands Avenue North. (R. F. Mack)

10. Two "Coronations", no. 111 leading, await the completion of repairs to the overhead on 26th September 1964. Note the sharpness of the curve from King Edward Street into Paragon Street, which was erected as part of the one-way system in June. Compare this view with the wartime photographs nos 4 and 5, taken in 1941. (C. W. Routh)

Service 63. King Edward Street—Endike Lane
via Beverley Road.

From KING EDWARD STREET.

Sunday	Monday to Friday		Saturday
a.m.	a.m.	a.m.	a.m.
9 20	* 5 30	11 21	* 5 30
9 40	* 6 0	11 27	* 6 0
10 0	* 6 20	11 33	* 6 20
and every	6 50	11 38	6 50
20 mins.	7 0	11 44	7 0
until	7 8	11 48	7 8
p.m.	7 13	11 52	7 13
1 0	7 18	and every	7 18
1 10	and every	3 and 4 mins.	and every
1 18	5 mins.	until	5 and 6 mins.
1 25	until	p.m.	until
1 32	8 18	4 18	8 42
1 39	8 21	4 21	8 47
1 46	8 25	and every	and every
1 53	and every	2 and 3 mins.	4 and 5 mins.
2 0	3 and 4 mins.	until	until
2 7	until	5 58	11 42
2 13	9 18	6 0	11 45
2 19	9 24	6 5	and every
2 25	9 30	6 10	2 and 3 mins.
2 31	9 36	6 15	until
2 36	9 42	6 20	5 59
and every	9 48	6 25	6 3
5 and 6 mins.	9 53	6 30	and every
until	9 59	6 35	4 and 5 mins.
10 0	10 5	6 40	until
10 5	10 11	6 45	10 16
10 10	10 17	6 50	10 21
10 15	10 23	6 55	10 25
10 20	10 28	7 0	10 29
10 25	10 34	7 5	10 34
10 30	10 40	7 10	10 38
10 35	10 46	and every	10 43
10 40	10 52	5 mins.	10 47
10 45 p.m.	10 58	until	10 51
	11 3	11 0	10 56
	11 9	p.m.	11 0
	11 15		p.m.

* Ser. 17 Motorbus

From ENDIKE LANE.

Sunday	Monday to Friday		Saturday
a.m.	a.m.	a.m.	a.m.
9 0	* 4 58	11 3	* 4 58
9 20	* 5 28	11 9	* 5 28
9 40	* 6 03	11 15	* 6 03
and every	6 30	11 20	6 30
20 mins.	6 40	11 26	6 40
until	6 50	11 30	6 50
p.m.	6 55	11 34	6 55
12 40	and every	11 37	7 0
12 50	5 mins.	and every	7 6
1 0	until	3 and 4 mins.	and every
1 7	8 0	until	5 and 6 mins.
1 14	8 3	4 0	until
1 21	8 7	p.m.	8 29
1 28	and every	4 3	8 34
1 35	3 and 4 mins.	and every	and every
1 42	until	2 and 3 mins.	4 and 5 mins.
1 49	8 56	until	until
1 55	9 0	5 43	11 24
2 2	9 6	5 47	11 27
2 8	9 12	5 52	and every
2 14	9 18	5 57	2 and 3 mins.
2 19	9 24	6 2	until
2 25	9 30	6 7	p.m.
and every	9 35	6 12	5 41
5 and 6 mins.	9 41	6 17	5 45
until	9 47	6 22	and every
10 3	9 53	6 27	4 and 5 mins.
10 8	9 59	6 32	until
10 13	10 5	6 37	9 58
10 18	10 10	6 42	10 3
10 23	10 16	6 47	10 7
10 28 p.m.	10 22	6 52	10 11
	10 28	6 57	10 16
	10 34	and every	10 20
	10 40	5 mins.	10 25
	10 45	until	10 29
	10 51	10 42	10 33
	10 57	p.m.	10 38
			10 42 p.m.

* Ser. 17 Motorbus

PROSPECT STREET

11.   In peak hours, Prospect Street was scheduled to have forty trolleybuses an hour on services 61/2/3 in each direction. All three vehicles are on service 62 so it appears that the Botanic Gardens and Stepney level crossings have disrupted the timetables for all three routes. Crossley no. 40, driven by Harold Blanchard, is leading the way from King Edward Street followed by Sunbeam W no. 72 and another Crossley, some time in December 1961. (R. F. Mack)

12.   Another collection of trolleybuses is caught by the camera in Prospect Street. This time, four are travelling towards King Edward Street past the new Central Library construction site, Sunbeam W no. 73 being the nearest vehicle. In the distance a "Coronation" is about to turn into Beverley Road. The section supply cables can be seen above no. 73. (R. F. Mack)

SPRING BANK

13.   By 7th November 1938, when this photograph was taken, the tram routes along Spring Bank had been replaced together with the Beverley Road route. Driver training is in full swing, possibly for the conversion of the Holderness Road route. A Crossley trolleybus is approaching the city centre on learner duties; the centre-grooved tram track is still in situ. The buildings on the left survive, but the *Hull Daily Mail* headquarters now occupy the area on the right. (KHCA)

14.   This photograph captures the scale of traffic delays resulting from the level crossing at Botanic Gardens, where services 61 and 62 parted company. Crossley no. 35, on service 65, is pulling away from the crossing where another Crossley is turning from Princes Avenue on service 62. Across the road the "Coronation" in the nearside lane is bound for Chanterlands Avenue, whilst the Brush-bodied Sunbeam W will turn right into Princes Avenue. (Authors' collections)

15. If there was an emergency in the city centre or a royal visit was in progress, services 61 and 62 were turned at Vine Street, a short distance from Ferensway. During such a visit on 19th May 1957 Crossley no. 41 has already been turned whilst another is reversing into Vane Street. Note the extreme angle of the trolley boom. Two more await their turn. (R. F. Mack)

Service 61. King Edward Street—Chanterlands Avenue North via Spring Bank West.

From KING EDWARD STREET

Sunday	Mon. to Fri.	Saturday
a.m.	a.m.	a.m.
9 20	5 15	5 15
and ev. 40	and ev. 30	and ev. 30
mins. until	mins. until	mins. until
p.m.	6 45	6 45
1 20	7 00	7 00
1 40	and ev. 7	and ev. 7
2 00	mins. until	mins. until
and ev. 10	8 19	9 18
mins. until	8 25	and ev. 9
4 40	and every 5	mins. until
4 48	mins. until	12 00
and every 12	9 00	and ev. 5/6
mins. until	9 12	mins. until
10 00	and ev. 12	p.m.
and ev. 9	mins. until	6 20
mins. until	12 00	and ev. 10
10 45	and ev. 7/8	mins. until
p.m.	mins. until	7 40
	7 40	7 48
	7 48	and every 12
	p.m.	mins. until
	2 24	9 48
	and ev. 9/10	and every 9
	mins. until	mins. until
	4 27	11 00
	and ev. 5/6	p.m.
	mins. until	
	6 12	
	and every 12	
	mins. until	
	11 00	
	p.m.	

From CHANTERLANDS AVENUE NORTH

Sunday	Mon. to Fri.	Saturday
a.m.	a.m.	a.m.
9 00	4 57	4 57
and ev. 40	5 30	5 30
mins. until	6 00	6 00
p.m.	6 30	6 30
1 00	6 45	6 45
1 40	6 49	6 49
and ev. 10	and ev. 7	and ev. 7
mins. until	mins. until	mins. until
4 30	8 00	8 20
and ev. 12	and ev. 5/6	8 26
mins. until	mins. until	8 32
8 49	8 49	8 38
9 42	8 58	8 45
9 51	9 6	8 52
10 00	and ev. 12	9 00
10 09	mins. until	and every 9
10 18	11 42	mins. until
10 27	and ev. 7/8	11 42
p.m.	mins. until	and ev. 5/6
	p.m.	mins. until
	2 05	p.m.
	and ev. 9/10	5 46
	mins. until	5 53
	4 08	6 02
	4 13	6 12
	and ev. 5/6	6 20
	mins. until	and every 10
	5 45	mins. until
	5 54	7 30
	and every 12	and every 12
	mins. until	mins. until
	10 42	10 06
	p.m.	and every 9
		mins. until
		10 42
		p.m.

Service 62. King Edward Street—Newland Avenue via Spring Bank and Prince's Avenue.

From KING EDWARD STREET.

Sunday	Monday to Friday	Saturday
a.m.	a.m.	a.m.
9 20	5 30	5 30
and every	6 0	6 0
20 mins.	6 15	6 15
until	6 30	6 30
1 20 p.m.	6 41	6 45
1 30	6 49	6 56
1 40	and every	and every
1 50	7 & 8 mins.	7 mins.
2 0	until	until
2 10	8 18	8 38
and every	8 24	and every
7 & 8 mins.	8 30	5 & 6 mins.
until	and every	until
10 27	4 mins.	11 48
10 33	until	11 52
10 39	9 06	and every
10 45	and every	4 mins.
p.m.	7 & 8 mins.	until
	until	9 06
	11 44	p.m.
	11 49	12 40
	and every	and every
	5 & 6 mins.	5 mins.
	until	until
	3 1	6 3
	and every	and every
	7 & 8 mins.	6 & 7 mins.
	until	until
	4 54	10 50
	and every	10 55
	4 mins.	11 0
	until	p.m.
	6 0	
	and every	
	7 & 8 mins.	
	until	
	11 0 p.m	

From NEWLAND AVENUE.

Sunday	Monday to Friday	Saturday
a.m.	a.m.	a.m.
* 7 5	5 15	5 15
9 0	5 45	5 45
and every	6 0	6 0
20 mins.	6 15	6 15
until	and every	and every
p.m.	7 mins.	7 mins.
1 0	until	until
1 10	8 6	8 20
1 20	8 12	and every
1 30	and every	5 & 6 mins
1 40	4 mins.	until
1 50	until	11 30
2 0	8 48	11 34
and every	and every	and every
7 & 8 mins.	7 & 8 mins.	4 mins.
until	until	until
10 27	11 31	12 22
p.m.	and every	and every
	5 & 6 mins.	5 and 6 mins.
	until	until
	2 50	7 52
	and every	and every
	7 & 8 mins.	7 & 8 mins.
	until	until
	4 36	9 04
	and every	and every
	4 mins. until	5 mins.
	5 40	until
	and every	10 37
	7 & 8 mins.	10 42
	until	p.m.
	10 30	
	10 36	
	10 42	
	p.m.	

* Ser. 22 Motorbus

Service 65. The route number "65" denotes additional trolleybuses on this service, running between King Edward Street and Goddard Avenue only.

Service 66. The route number "66" denotes additional trolleybuses on this service running between King Edward Street and Pearson Park only.

16. Crossley no. 33 passes the well-known Duggleby's toy and cycle shop as it leaves Spring Bank West and prepares to join the service 62 overhead at the Botanic Gardens crossing. In the background another Crossley enters Spring Bank West. (R. F. Mack)

17. The murky weather suggests Christmas time is the reason for this service 66 working by Sunbeam W no. 81. The trolleybus is gliding past the policeman on point duty as it turns into Princes Avenue.(R. F. Mack)

18. Overhead linemen Bill Kent and Paddy Reid watch closely as "Coronation" no. 103 approaches the turnout near Stanley Street on 6th August 1960. No. 103 will take the nearside set of wires, service 62 trolleybuses continuing straight on. The overhead line section was divided into three shifts and each one was responsible for two of the six routes in operation. JKH 682 is the Karrier tower wagon which dated from 1948. (R. F. Mack)

SPRING BANK WEST

19. This appears to be, at first glance, a routine photograph of "Coronation" no. 110 at the junction of Spring Bank West and Chanterlands Avenue. In fact, there are two sets of overhead wires in view, both of which turn into Chanterlands Avenue. The date is not recorded but no. 110 looks fairly new so it could be some time in 1955. The outside wires appear to be new and it may be that these will shortly be brought into use, perhaps to reduce the travel arc of the booms. This will minimise the possibility of the retriever ropes fouling other traffic. (R.F.Mack)

20. On 19th October 1957, Crossley no. 31 waits as its load of fairgoers alights at the temporary stop in Spring Bank West. This stop was provided to ease the congestion in Chanterlands Avenue South during Hull Fair week. The conductor's five chamber Ultimate ticket machine is easily seen as the he supervises the unloading. Throughout the week trolleybuses on services 61 and 69, which served the other end of Walton Street from Anlaby Road, carried the "TO THE FAIR" sticker in the position shown. (R. F. Mack)

21. Sunbeam W no. 86, driven by Motorman Ron Gould, is collecting passengers at the first stop after leaving Chanterlands Avenue. Behind no. 86 is one of the three cemeteries along the route all of which generated considerable traffic on Sunday afternoons and bank holidays. This would compensate for the relatively low passenger levels on services 61 and 65. (D. F. Parker)

CHANTERLANDS AVENUE

22.   The relatively quiet Chanterlands Avenue route came alive every year during Hull Fair week, when a large number of additional journeys were provided as far as Chanterlands Avenue South. On 15th October 1960, Crossley no. 41, having arrived from King Edward Street, makes the awkward turn across the carriageway. It was rarely possible for the turn to be completed in a single attempt, so some skilful manoeuvering was required. All turns were carried out under supervision, Chief Inspector E. (Teddy) Milligan being in charge on this occasion. (A. D. Packer)

23.   Also during Hull Fair week on 14th October 1961, three trolleybuses are pictured at Chanterlands Avenue South. The leading "Coronation", no. 105 is travelling the full route to Chanterlands Avenue North, but no. 116, immediately behind, is unusually employed on the short working. It will shortly make the awkward turn across the reservation before returning to the city centre. (Vectis Transport Publications)

No. 61 & 65 TROLLEY BUS SERVICES					
Stage.					
1.				Hull (King Edward Street)	
2.	2d.			Hutt Street	
3.	3d.	2d.		Hymers Avenue	
4.	4d.	3d.	2d.	Chanterlands Avenue South	
5.	4d.	3d.	3d.	2d.	Bricknell Avenue
6.	5d.	4d.	4d.	3d.	2d. Chanterlands Ave. North

Special Fare: Chanterlands Avenue North to Cottingham Road
Garage—2d. (Children at 3 and under 14 years—1d.

No. 62 & 66 TROLLEY BUS SERVICES				
Stage.				
1.				Hull (King Edward Street)
2.	2d.			Hutt Street
3.	3d.	2d.		Park Avenue
4.	4d.	3d.	2d.	Alexandra Road
5.	5d.	4d.	3d.	2d. Newland Avenue (Cottingham Road)

No. 63 TROLLEY BUS SERVICE				
Stage.				
1.				Hull (King Edward Street)
2.	2d.			Wellington Lane
3.	3d.	2d.		Washington Street or De Grey Street
4.	4d.	3d.	2d.	Haworth Street
5.	5d.	4d.	3d.	2d. Endike Lane (Beverley High Road)

No. 64 & 68 TROLLEY BUS SERVICES				
Stage.				
1.				Hull (Jameson Street)
2.	2d.			Cleveland Street
3.	3d.	2d.		Craven Street
4.	4d.	3d.	2d.	Summergangs Road.
5.	5d.	4d.	3d.	2d. Ings Road (Holderness Road)

24.   Photographs of Sunbeam F4s on the Chanterlands Avenue service are rare, neither author possessing a single view of an F4 on service 61. So this picture of no. 92 on a service 65 working is noteworthy, to say the least. The number "5" is much cleaner than the "6", having seen little use.(R. F. Mack)

25.   Sunbeam W no. 79 travels along Chanterlands Avenue towards Goddard Avenue with feeder equipment in the background. No. 79 was withdrawn when services 61/5 were abandoned on 28th July 1962. (Authors' collections)

26.   On a wintry day Sunbeam W no. 80 passes the vacant Goddard Avenue short working loop and makes its way to "town". Few passengers are on board (not unusual on this section) and there are no pedestrians in sight. When originally introduced in 1937, all off-peak journeys worked to Goddard Avenue only, as service 61A, with the full route operating only at peaks and late evening. This was revived for a time in 1957, but did not last long due to the lack of passengers on this section. (R. F. Mack)

27.	Another view of Goddard Avenue, this time on a sunny 21st August 1961, shows Sunbeam W no. 86 waiting in the loop whilst "Coronation" no. 107 unloads across the road. We are afforded a good view of the impressive rear of no. 107 and its trolley retrievers. (R. F. Mack)

28.	Crossley no. 31 waits in the Goddard Avenue turning circle, whilst city-bound no. 32 passes. The date is 6th October 1961 and both trolleybuses appear to be in good external condition despite having only three months of service remaining. (R. F. Mack)

29.   On 24th September 1959, "Coronation" no. 103, driven by Motorman Clive Fisher passes an inward-bound Crossley (no. 39) on Chanterlands Avenue North. The photograph provides a good view of the painted-over rear destination box on no. 39. Use of rear destination displays was abandoned around 1947. Some trolleybuses received flush panels in replacement, but most boxes were painted over. The photograph also shows the more suburban nature of the last part of the route. It was taken by Les Storry who worked at Cottingham Road Garage for many years and was a fervent enthusiast. (L. R. Storry)

——————▶

30.   From time to time trolleybuses were loaned to other garages, although the parent garage remained responsible for maintenance. Nevertheless, it was unusual for a TB7 to work away from Holderness Road and this is a rare view of no. 65 at the terminus. Also in view is the white line painted on the fence to assist motormen to position their vehicle at the barrier without blocking the drive of a house. In the background is a "Coronation" (no. 113) on a test run.(A. D. Packer)

——————▶

31.   Leyland TB4 no. 8 was one of the first batch that inaugurated the Chanterlands Avenue route in July 1937. Fifteen years later, no. 8 is still employed on service 61 and is waiting at the last setting down point before crossing the reservation to the outward stop. It carries an advertisement for Vernons pools which crosses the curve of the streamline livery. This is unusual since the forward part of such advertisements normally followed the curve and did not intrude on the white area. (Authors' collections)

32.   Saturday, 28th July 1962, was a warm and sunny day and Sunbeam W no. 72 is caught sunning itself at the Chanterlands Avenue North terminus. Today will be its last day in service and, in the early evening, it will be towed to Liverpool Street to await sale and scrapping. Radiussed rubber mountings have been fitted to the upper deck front windows and destination box. Note how the top part of the advertisement panel follows the curve of the livery.
(M. J. Wells)

33.   A turning circle was provided at the end of the short dual carriageway section at Chanterlands Avenue North. This was used by trolleybuses on test from Cottingham Road Garage and, as here, by trainee motormen. "Coronation" no. 109 is standing at this circle which was used by wartime service 67 to turn back to the city centre. The date is 30th July 1959. (R. F. Mack)

COTTINGHAM ROAD

34.   Cottingham Road's overhead wires ran from Beverley Road past the garage, Newland Avenue and the Teacher Training College to Chanterlands Avenue North. As previously mentioned, it was used for garage workings, testing vehicles and by learner vehicles. Hull did not possess a dedicated learner vehicle, preferring to use ordinary trolleybuses. "Coronation" no. 109 is seen on such a duty as it turns into Chanterlands Avenue North from Cottingham Road on 30th July 1959. Wartime service no. 67 would made such a turn as it completed its journey from King Edward Street. (Authors' collections)

35.   Two "Coronations", the nearest being no. 110 approach the entrance to Cottingham Road garage after completing their tours of duty. This view affords a good view of the impressive rear end of the MF2Bs. Just in view on the left is the "temporary" Traffic Office which lasted from 1941 until the opening of the new central offices in 1960. (C. W.Routh).

36. Driver training, which continued until the Spring of 1964, involved a course comprising several days theory followed by driving lessons using different classes of trolleybuses under supervision. Once a trainee had satisfied the instructor that he was capable of driving a trolleybus, he was given a blue card which permitted him to drive a service trolleybus under the supervision of the rostered motorman. A record was made of each such journey and eventually the trainee would undertake a full test. On 4 July 1962, Sunbeam W no. 82 was posed opposite Cottingham Road Garage whilst on training duty. (R. F. Mack)

37. Crossley no. 38 is about to leave "Cott Road" as Cottingham Road Garage was known locally, to take up service on Beverley Road. The date is 1st April 1960 which is probably a Sunday, as journeys before 1.00pm were often worked by Crossleys rather than the usual MF2Bs. (M.I.Baxter)

PRINCES AVENUE

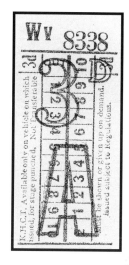

38.   Leyland TB4 no. 23 is seen amongst the shopping area on the lower part of Princes Avenue en route to Newland Avenue. The Weymann bodies were built to a neat and compact design, which was helped by the way in which the trolley gantries were incorporated within the overall roof line. (Authors' collections)

39.   On days immediately preceding bank holidays and the Christmas and New Year periods, additional journeys were operated on short workings 65/66/71. On 3rd December 1960, two Crossleys are caught at the Pearson Park turning circle. No. 41 is working a Christmas extra whilst no. 37 is on the main service 62. No other scheduled workings were made to this point. The turning area still exists but is unused. (A. D. Packer)

40. Another pre-Bank Holiday working found "Coronation" no. 115 on service 66. On 31st August 1962 no. 115 is passing the final parade of shops on Princes Avenue and its next stop will be at the Pearson Park turning circle. (Vectis Transport Publications)

41. The character of Princes Avenue changed completely, north of Blenheim Street, as shops and densely-packed streets gave way to the "Avenues". This was a prosperous area of solid Victorian housing along the main road and the five avenues that ran between here and Chanterlands Avenue. Sunbeam W no. 77 glides past the turning circle at Pearson Park on its way to the city centre. (R. F. Mack)

42. Sunbeam W no. 81 is seen at the northern end of the avenue with a reasonable load on board. The "relaxed" utility style of the bodywork can be clearly seen. (Authors' collections)

43. The Queens Hotel frames Roe-bodied Sunbeam W no. 83, as it prepares to turn across the wide junction from Queens Road into Princes Avenue. This was an important junction for KHCT passengers. Service 62 connected with motorbus services 26/27, which ran between the Fish Dock in the south and the industrial area of Bankside alongside the River Hull, and with service 28 which started at the bus stop outside the public house in Princes Road and ran to Chapman Street in East Hull. The 27 and 28 ran at peaks and on Saturday mornings, catering mainly for office and factory workers. For many years a special transfer ticket was available on service 62 for transfer to and use on the 27 and 28. (R. F. Mack)

44. The turn from Princes Avenue into Queens Road was a fairly tight one but the motorman in charge of Leyland no.23 appears to be experiencing little difficulty. No. 23 has received the later Gill Sans style fleet number. (R. F. Mack)

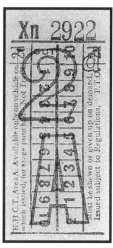

NEWLAND AVENUE

45. In May 1941 all trolleybuses had their areas of white paint overpainted in blue to eliminate the possibility of their being spotted by enemy aircraft on moonlit nights. The entire process was carried out inside ten days and the result can be clearly seen on Crossley TDD4 no. 28 at the junction of Cottingham Road and Newland Avenue in July 1945. No. 28 also displays the large service number blinds that were introduced in the early part of 1942 to assist passengers to identify individual services in the blackout. Note the wartime headlamp arrangement. (Omnibus Society)

46. Following cessation of hostilities in Europe, the Transport Department was able to resume re-painting of its fleet, albeit on a limited scale. Leyland TB4 no. 22 was the first trolleybus to be repainted and to receive the revised post-war livery, which omitted the word "HULL" above the lower deck and eliminated the central white band. The legend "CORPORATION TRANSPORT" in gold lettering was placed within a white rectangle, which was subsequently rounded off. In June 1945 the newly painted no. 22 was posed for photographs in Cottingham Road opposite the traffic office and near the garage. (KHCA)

47. The 1947 Sunbeam Ws were initially allocated to Cottingham Road but were subsequently moved to Hessle Road and Wheeler Street. In 1961 some returned to Cottingham Road, one of which being no. 86 which is seen awaiting departure time in charge of Motorman Ron Gould. Newland Avenue was an exclusive trolleybus domain, the only diesel working being an early Sunday morning works service. (Authors' collections)

48.   On 18th May 1959 crowds were gathering to attend the annual Whit Monday gala at the Sailors' Orphans Homes complex, which was located opposite the service 62 terminus. Sunbeam W no. 74 is leaving for the city centre and is overtaking another Sunbeam W, which has its trolleybooms pinned down. An attendance of 20,000 people was usual and trolleybuses (and motorbuses) were borrowed from other garages to assist with the movement of passengers between lunchtime and early evening. (Authors' collections)

49.   The stop opposite the Monica cinema was used by Malcolm when visiting relatives who lived in a street off the western side of Newland Avenue. This photograph shows the trolleybus stop (white lettering on a green background) and the fare stage indication (red lettering on a white background). Motorbus stop signs had blue lettering. The trolleybus, "Coronation" no. 109 is in the charge of Motorman Bob Gaffney and he has just two more stops before reaching the terminus. (Authors' collections)

50. Throughout the 1950s, the Crossleys were the mainstay of service 62. They were not displaced until January 1962, when the remaining class members were moved to service 69. They were eventually withdrawn. No. 33 and an unidentified sister vehicle await departure time in an often repeated scene at the terminus, one which Malcolm witnessed most nights after school. (Authors' collections)

51.   The Monica cinema can be seen in the background, as Sunbeam W no. 82 passes the William Jackson store at the top of Grafton Street on its way to the city centre. Motorman John Allen, who is in charge, was a regular contributor to the local press about KHCT in the fifties and sixties.
(Vectis Transport Publications)

→

52.   In 1963, eight Atlanteans were ordered for the conversion of service 62 in the Autumn of 1964. However, following the completion of a repair programme on Hull's large fleet of AEC Regents, it was decided to use ten of these to replace the Newland Avenue route as soon as possible. So unexpected was this decision, that Sunbeam F4s nos 97 and 100 had just been repainted in anticipation of a further year's service. No. 95 is seen here on 2nd October 1963, just six weeks before withdrawal on 16th November 1963. (J. C. Gillham)

No. 47			No. 50			TROLLEY BUS SERVICES				No. 61a		No. 62	
						No. 61							
City	Term.	City Term.	City		Term.		Chants.			City	Godd.	City	New.
a.m.	a.m.	**Saturday**	a.m.	p.m.	a.m. p.m.	City	North	**Saturdays**	a.m.	a.m.	Ave.		Ave.
4 45	5 0	From	5 5¶	4 20	6 5¶ 5 10	a.m.	a.m.	City Term.	a.m.	a.m.	a.m. a.m.	a.m. a.m.
5 0	5 15	a.m. a.m.	6 15¶	4 30¶	7 35¶ 5 30	5 15	4 57	From	6 45	7 0	5 15 5 0
5 15	5 30	9 10 9 20	7 40¶	4 40	7 55¶ 5 50	5 30	5 15	1140 1144	6 52	7 8	5 30 5 15
5 30	5 45	approx.	8 0	5 0	8 10 6 10*	5 45	5 30	every	7 0	7 16	5 45 5 30
5 45	6 0	every	8 10¶	5 0¶	8 30 6 25¶	6 0	5 45	5 mins.	7 8	7 24	6 0 5 45
5 52	6 6	5 mins.	8 20	5 20	8 50 6 30*	6 15	6 0	until	7 12	7 30	6 15 6 0
6 0	6 12	until	8 40	5 40	8 55¶ 6 50*	6 30	6 15	p.m. p.m.	See 61		6 30 6 15
every			9 0	6 0	9 10 7 10*	6 45	6 30	11 0 1043	8 52 9 8		6 38 6 30
5 mins.		p.m. p.m.	9 0¶	6 20*	9 25¶ 7 30*	6 16	6 34		9 0 9 16		6 45
until		11 0 1042	9 20	6 40*	9 50 7 50*	7 24	6 45	**Sunday**	every		every
a.m. a.m.		**Sunday**	9 40	6 45¶	1045¶ 8 5¶	7 30	6 50	a.m. a.m.	8 mins.		3 mins.
9 10 9 20		a.m. a.m.	10 0	7 0*	1120¶ 8 30*	7 35	6 54	9 20 9 5	until		until
every		9 30 9 10	10 0¶	7 20*	1210 8 50*	7 40	7 14	every	p.m. p.m.		a.m. a.m.
10 mins.		every	11 0¶	7 40*	1230 9 10*	7 45	7 34	20 mins.	10 0 10 0		9 0 9 0
until		20 mins.	1130¶	8 0*	1250 9 15¶	7 50	7 37	until	10 6 10 6		then
a.m. a.m.		until	12 0	8 20*	1 10 9 30*	every		p.m. p.m.	1012 1012		every
1130 1150		p.m. p.m.	1220	8 30¶	1 30 9 35¶	3 to 4 mins.		1 0 1 0	1018 1018		3 to 5 mins.
every		1250 1250	1240	8 40*	1 50 9 50*	until		every	1024 1024		until
5 mins.		1257 1 0	1245¶	9 0*	1 50¶ 1010*	9 0 9 12		6 mins.	See 61		p.m. p.m.
until		approx.	1 0	9 20*	2 10* 1030*	See 61a		until			11 0 1044
10 0 9 30		every	1 10¶	9 40*	2 10¶ 1050*	1148 1142		p.m. p.m.	**Sundays**		
10 8 9 40		5 mins.	1 20	9 40¶	2 30* 1045¶	every		4 42 4 24	See		**Sunday**
1016 9 50		until	1 40	10 0*	2 50*	4 mins.		every	No. 61		a.m. a.m.
1024 10 0		p.m. p.m.	2 0	1020*	3 10* **Sun.**	2 20 2 42		7 mins.			9 30 9 15
1032 1010		1030 10 4	2 5¶	1040*	3 30* 9 20¶	every		until			9 50 9 35
1040 1020		.. ..	2 20*		3 35¶ 1125¶	6 mins.		p.m. p.m.			every
1048 1028		.. ..	2 25¶	**Suns.**	3 50* 2 35¶	until		1020 10 1			20 mins.
1054 1036		.. ..	2 40*	1035¶	3 55¶ 4 45¶	4 22 4 4					until
11 0 1042		.. ..	3 0*	1 45¶	4 10 5 45¶	every					p.m. p.m.
.. ..		.. ..	3 20*	3 55¶	4 30 6 45¶	4 mins.					1250 1255
.. ..		.. ..	3 40*	4 55¶	4 45* 1040¶	until					1 10 1 5
.. ..		.. ..	3 45¶	5 55¶	.. ..	6 36 6 46					every
.. ..		.. ..	4 0	9 5¶		See 61a					5 mins.
.. ..		.. ..			¶ Additional Buses in	1030 ..					until
.. ..		.. ..			connection with Boats.	1036 ..					p.m. p.m.
.. ..		.. ..			* Saturdays only.	1042 ..					1020 10 4
.. ..		.. ..				1048 ..					
.. ..		.. ..				1054 ..					
No						11 0 ..					

¶ Additional Buses in connection with Boats.
* Saturdays only.

BEVERLEY ROAD

53.   The twenty Crossley TDD4s, purchased for the opening of the Beverley Road route in October 1938, were in daily use on the route 63 until the "Coronations" took over in May 1955. No. 33 is seen here in May 1953 at Endike Lane. (J. Fozard)

54.   On Sunday mornings, service 63 was often worked by conventional trolleybuses. This was done to ensure that crews remained familiar with other types and their operating characteristics. Sunbeam W no. 78 approaches Blundell's Corner in either 1961 or 1962. (R.F.Mack)

55.   Crew changes on the Beverley Road route took place at the stop opposite Haworth Street, which was a two minute stroll from Cottingham Road Garage. The changeover is taking place whilst no. 108 and its passengers wait patiently. Motorman BonTempo is leaving the cab whilst Jim Cook is about to assume charge. Readers may notice that Motorman Cook is wearing cycle clips, something that many did in order to offset the drafts for which "Coronation" cabs were noted. (Authors' collections)

56. The Stepney level crossing lies behind the photographer and is the reason for this queue of traffic on Beverley Road on 5th October 1959. "Coronation" no. 106 leads the line-up of two further "Coronations" plus two Weymann-bodied AEC Reliances and an East Yorkshire Roe bodied "Yellow Peril" Leyland Titan. (R. F. Mack)

---

57. Beyond Inglemire Lane, the Beverley Road route became more suburban and less densely populated. Had a suitable turning point existed in 1952 when short running was introduced on certain routes, including the Holderness Road route, alternate off-peak journeys would have terminated near this point. The prototype "Coronation", no. 101, is leaving the dual carriageway section en route for King Edward Street in March 1961. No. 101 carries advertisements for local brewery Moors and Robson's mild and bitter beers. Similar adverts for Hull Brewery and Darleys were carried from time to time by several trolleybuses. (Authors' collections)

58. Motorman McKindo and his conductor observe the photographer at the Endike Lane terminus on 16th September 1958. The photograph provides a clear view of the full-length periscope installed on the upper deck of no. 101 to assist motormen with assessing occupancy of the upper saloon in connection with one-man operation plans. Only no. 101 possessed the full length version, but this was replaced with the modified version around 1960. (L. R. Storry)

59. Sunbeam W no. 80 stands at the terminus in pre-"Coronation" days. No. 80 was Hull's longest lived trolleybus, despite being withdrawn in September 1963 when eighteen years old. It was discovered in a Bingley scrapyard in 1972, but it was in too poor a condition to be worthy of preservation. (Authors' collections)

60. Perhaps the most complicated overhead junction on the system was that which connected Cottingham Road with Beverley Road. The triangular installation permitted trolleybuses to turn both ways into Beverley Road and to reach the garage from either direction. On 2nd October 1963, no. 111 is bound for Endike Lane, whilst no. 104, in the background, is inward bound.
(J. C. Gillham)

HOLDERNESS ROAD

61.   Leyland TB7 no. 52 leaves North Bridge and enters Witham on its way to Ings Road. The overhead was encased in wooden troughs located on the centre of the bridge, which forced trolleybuses to cross it in the centre at the regulation speed of 5 mph. Trolleybuses on the Holderness Road route were equipped with specially constructed (in Liverpool Street Works) larger trolleyheads in order to negotiate the bridge. (R. F. Mack)

62.   When, in the late fifties, the first Leyland TB7s were withdrawn, some Crossleys were sent from Cottingham Road to Holderness Road to assist with maintaining the service. Crossley no.44 is shown crossing the reservation to reach the inward stop at the Ings Road terminus. (R. F. Mack)

63.   Leyland TB7 no. 61 is seen outside Holderness Road Garage on 28th August 1955. Shortly after this photograph was taken, the entry and exit arrangements were reversed so that trolleybuses used the narrow side road before swinging right to enter the garage and leaving by the overhead immediately above no. 61. This arrangement brought back the original overhead layout of 1939. For some reason the trolleybus on the opposite side of the road has its booms lowered. (R. F. Mack)

64.   The Leyland TB7s operated the Holderness Road route from February 1940 until transfer
to Hessle Road in January 1961. Sometime in 1960, no. 54 leads no. 55 towards the Southcoates
level crossing. Although delivered in the late Summer of 1939, no. 54 was stored at Cottingham
Road until service 64 became operational in February 1940. (R. F. Mack)

65. On a busy sunny day, Sunbeam F4 no. 95, looking in good condition, is city bound as it approaches the Southcoates level crossing. Two other Roe-bodied Sunbeams approach the railway bridge. (R. F. Mack)

Service 64. Paragon Square—Ings Road via Holderness Road

From PARAGON SQUARE

Sunday	Monday to Friday	Saturday
a.m.	a.m.	a.m.
9 20	5 18	5 18
9 40	5 30	5 30
10 00	5 54	5 54
10 20	6 18	6 18
10 40	6 30	6 30
11 00	6 42	6 48
11 20	6 50	6 54
& every 10	& every 5	7 00
mins. until	mins. until	& every 5
p.m.	8 10	mins. until
1 00	8 18	8 45
1 09	8 25	8 55
1 20	8 31	9 04
1 27	& every 3	& every 8
1 35	mins. until	mins. until
1 42	9 05	11 50
1 50	mins. until	p.m.
& every 5	4 15	12 32
mins. until	& every 6	& every 3 or
9 10	mins. until	4 mins. until
9 20	5 33	4 31
9 25	mins. until	& every 6
9 35	5 59	mins. until
9 44	6 05	5 49
9 52	6 13	mins. until
10 06	6 21	7 07
10 08	6 29	mins. until
& every 4	mins. until	7 37
mins. until	7 25	7 42
10 40	& every 5	& every 3
10 45 p.m.	mins. until	mins. until
	10 00	8 26
	& every 4	& every 5 or
	mins. until	6 mins. until
	11 00 p.m.	10 21
		& every 3
		mins. until
		11 00 p.m.

From INGS ROAD

Sunday	Monday to Friday	Saturday
a.m.	a.m.	a.m.
6 58	4 55	4 55
9 00	5 12	5 12
& every 20	5 36	5 36
mins. until	5 53	5 53
11 00	6 00	6 00
& every 10	6 12	6 12
mins. until	6 24	6 24
p.m.	6 30	6 30
1 00	& every 5	6 36
1 07	mins. until	& every 5
1 15	8 00	mins. until
1 22	8 03	6 42
1 30	& every 6	6 45
& every 5	mins. until	& every 5
mins. until	8 45	mins. until
9 25	& every 5	8 30
& every 8	mins. until	8 54
mins. until	p.m.	9 00
10 21	1 00	& every 8
10 26 p.m.	& every 6	mins. until
	mins. until	11 24
	2 40	11 28
	& every 5	& every 6
	mins. until	mins. until
	p.m.	p.m.
	12 50	4 15
	& every 6	& every 3 or
	mins. until	4 mins. until
	4 45	4 45
	& every 6	& every 6
	mins. until	mins. until
	6 47	6 05
	& every 4	& every 3
	mins. until	mins. until
	7 35	7 21
	& every 5	& every 5 or
	mins. until	6 mins. until
	10 10	10 39
	10 14	10 42 p.m.
	10 20	
	10 27	
	10 36	
	10 42 p.m.	

: Ser. 56 Motorbus
• Ser. 58 Motorbus

Service 68. Paragon Square—East Park via Holderness Rd.
Consolidated time-table of Services 64 and 68.

From PARAGON SQUARE

Sunday	Monday to Friday	Saturday
a.m.	a.m.	a.m.
9 20	5 18	5 18
9 40	5 30	5 30
10 00	5 54	5 54
10 20	6 18	6 18
10 40	6 30	6 30
11 00	6 42	6 48
11 20	6 50	6 54
& every 10	6 54	7 00
mins. until	& every 5	& every 10
p.m.	mins. until	mins. until
1 00	8 15	p.m.
1 09	& every 3	8 03
1 20	mins. until	& every 3
1 35	9 05	& every 3 &
1 42	p.m.	4 mins. until
1 50	8 20	p.m.
& every 5	p.m.	& every 5
mins. until	1 20	mins. until
9 40	& every 4	9 28
& every 4	mins. until	& every 4
mins. until	3 00	mins. until
10 40	& every 5	10 28 p.m.
10 45 p.m.	mins. until	11 00 p.m.
	4 10	
	& every 3	
	mins. until	
	5 57	
	& every 4	
	mins. until	
	7 25	
	& every 5	
	mins. until	
	10 00	
	& every 4	
	mins. until	
	11 00 p.m.	

From EAST PARK

Sunday	Monday to Friday	Saturday
a.m.	a.m.	a.m.
6 58	4 58	4 58
9 03	5 15	5 15
9 23	5 39	5 39
9 43	5 56	5 56
10 03	6 03	6 03
10 23	6 15	6 12
10 43	6 27	6 27
11 03	6 33	6 33
& every 10	6 39	6 45
mins. until	6 45	& every 5
p.m.	& every 5	mins. until
1 03	mins. until	8 50
1 10	8 03	& every 3
1 18	& every 3	& 4 mins.
1 25	mins. until	until
& every 5	p.m.	p.m.
mins. until	9 30	9 18
9 28	& every 4	& every 3
& every 4	mins. until	mins. until
mins. until	2 43	10 45 p.m.
2 43	& every 5	
& every 5	mins. until	
mins. until	3 48	
3 48	& every 3	
& every 3	mins. until	
mins. until	5 49	
5 49	& every 4	
& every 4	mins. until	
mins. until	7 38	
7 38	& every 5	
& every 5	mins. until	
mins. until	9 43	
9 43	& every 4	
& every 4	mins. until	
mins. until	10 45 p.m.	
10 45 p.m.		

: Ser. 56 Motorbus
• Ser. 58 Motorbus

66.   Sunbeam W no. 75, having been displaced from service 70, awaits departure time at the Ings Road terminus on 19th April 1961. No. 75 has received sliding vents in place of half drop opening windows and has lost its upper deck front quarter lights. Additionally, the destination box has received rubber mounted radiussed ends. (D. Tate)

67.   Trolleybuses which left Holderness Road Garage for the Ings Road terminus had to turn left from the garage before turning right across the central reservation. Crossley no. 35 has just completed this manoeuvre before travelling the short distance to Ings Road. (R. F. Mack)

68.   On Sunday 15th November 1959 the Doncaster Omnibus and Light Railway Society hired "Coronation" no. 115 for the only known trolleybus tour of the system. No. 115, which had just been repainted, was in excellent condition and was driven by Driving Instructor Geoff Smith. The tour covered the entire system and brought a "Coronation" to roads along which they did not usually work service journeys. This included Jameson Street where it is seen passing the Hammonds store, complete with Christmas decorations. (Authors' collections)

69. During the last few weeks of the Holderness Road route's life the five remaining 1945/6 Sunbeam Ws were transferred from Cottingham Road. On the last day, 21st September 1963, no. 84, which will also be withdrawn, is passing Laburnum Avenue en route for Ings Road. A 1947 Sunbeam W is inward bound on the opposite side of the road. (C. W. Routh)

70. Later that night, at 11.20pm, Motorman Charles Kerris brings an empty no. 90 to a halt outside Holderness Road Garage having completed the final service 64 journey and travelled the short distance from the Ings Road terminus. No. 90 and those trolleybuses that can be seen inside the garage will soon be towed across the city centre to Liverpool Street and sale. (L. R. Storry)

PARAGON STREET (WATERWORKS STREET)

71.   The city centre termini for services 69 and 70 were located in Paragon Street (called Waterworks Street until 1952). Leyland TB4 no. 19 is at the front of a row of three trolleybuses. No. 19 appears to be filling up quickly and those passengers in view will probably have to take the vehicle behind. At this time there was only a single loop for both services which tended to delay things, especially as motormen did not always take the inside siding. Two separate sidings would shortly be installed. (London Trolleybus Preservation Society)

No. 69 & 71 TROLLEY BUS SERVICES			
Stage.			
1.			Hull (Paragon Street)
2.	2d.		Linnaeus Street
3.	3d.	2d.	Walton Street
4.	4d.	3d.	2d. Meadowbank Road
No. 70 TROLLEY BUS SERVICE			
Stage.			
1.			Hull (Paragon Street)
2.	2d.		Alfred Street
3.	3d.	2d.	Division Road
4.	4d.	3d.	2d. Carlton Street

72. At Christmas time in 1960, Sunbeam W no. 71 glides effortlessly away from the service 70 barrier, leaving no. 74 to await its own departure time. One month later service 70 would be operated by motorbuses. (Douglas F. Parker)

73. When service 63 was re-routed in June 1964, the final setting down stop was located outside the City Hall in Paragon Street. "Coronation" no. 115 is pictured at that stop on 25th October 1964 during the last week of trolleybus operation. (M. J. Wells)

CARR LANE

74.   The last setting down stop for services 69 and 70 was situated under the City Hall and outside Sydney Scarborough's record shop in Carr Lane. There were no traction poles along this section of Carr Lane, so rosettes (called wall plates on some official drawings) were used for securing the overhead. These can be seen in this photograph above Sunbeam W no. 71 on service 69. Behind is a Sunbeam F4 on service 70. (C. Carter)

75.   Carr Lane was used in the opposite direction by service 64 and service 68 trolleybuses until March 1959, although the overhead was not dismantled until February 1962. Leyland TB7 no. 57 is entering Carr Lane from Queen Victoria Square. The service 69/70 inward wires are on the left. (R. F. Mack)

Nº AF 9ᴬ28

KINGSTON UPON HULL
CITY TRANSPORT

Prepaid 2p Fare

Available for Scholars over 14 years
and under 16 years of age, between
7-30 a.m. and 7-0 p.m. Not available Saturdays, Sundays and Holidays. This Ticket to be given to
the Operator in exchange for a
punched 2p ticket.

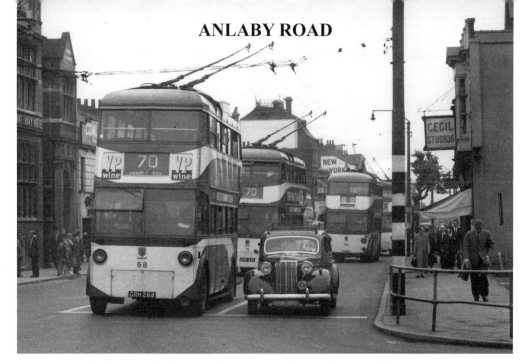

76.   Four trolleybuses wait for the traffic lights at the junction of Anlaby Road and Ferensway to change to allow them to reach Paragon Street. Sunbeam Ws no. 68, with upper deck quarter lights removed, and no. 71 are working service 70, whilst an F4 is on service 69. The presence of a Crossley behind the F4 suggests that this is a match day and, therefore, a Saturday. (R. F Mack)

77.   The overhead in Carr Lane was shared between the outward western trolleybus services and the inward Holderness Road services. Both Leyland TB7 no. 55 and Sunbeam F4 no. 94 have taken the straight wires, the inside set being for service 70. (London Trolleybus Preservation Society)

78. Towards the end of its working life, Leyland TB4 no. 18 is seen in a long queue on Anlaby Road, near the Boulevard level crossing. At this date (19th June 1954) no. 24 still carried a wartime service number only blind above the platform. (R. F. Mack)

79. The large number of rugby league fans in evidence suggests that it must be a Saturday, when Hull RLFC are at home at the "Boulevard". In order to assist with the movement of fans to and from the match, Crossley no. 43 has been borrowed from Cottingham Road. After unloading its passengers, it is about to turn into the Boulevard and travel the short distance to Malm Street, where it will use the reverser before returning to the city centre. Journey time was approximately seven minutes, the round trip taking less than fifteen minutes which enabled each vehicle to work three or four specials an hour before the match. (R. F. Mack)

80. Few motormen liked the reverser at Malm Street and dewirements were not unknown. Also, trolleybuses sometimes overshot the overhead in Boulevard, there being no markers to guide them, so that they had to be pushed back towards the wires! The manoeuvre was made under the supervision of an inspector but accidents still occurred. Here no. 89's motorman is about to reverse into Malm Street across the corner of the pavement and will probably demolish the police "NO PARKING" sign! The inspector, is Geoff Smith who drove no. 115 on the tour seen in photograph no. 68. (R. F. Mack)

81.   With its destination blind poorly set to show the service number only, Brush-bodied Sunbeam W no. 76 accelerates away from the Boulevard level crossing on Anlaby Road. The date is probably some time in 1961. This crossing was replaced with a road bridge in 1963. (John Fozard)

82.   Leyland TB4 no.18 basks in the sunshine at the Meadowbank Road terminus in the early fifties. This was a most popular location for photographs and the Hull Co-operative Society's shop in the background was probably the most photographed shop in the city. (R. F. Mack)

83. Sunbeam F4 no. 94 demonstrates the awkward turn out of the narrow lane that led from the Wheeler Street garage exit. Part of the Newington level crossing can be seen. When service 69 was introduced, it terminated at the nearby roundabout and no left hand curve was provided, trolleybuses proceeding direct to the city centre. When a short extension was constructed in March 1947, this curve was installed. (R. F. Mack)

Service 69. Paragon Street—Meadowbank Road
via Anlaby Road.

From PARAGON STREET			From MEADOWBANK ROAD		
Sunday	Monday to Friday	Saturday	Sunday	Monday to Friday	Saturday
a.m.	a.m.	a.m.	a.m.	a.m.	a.m.
9 20	5 15	5 15	9 0	5 0	5 0
9 40	* 5 45	* 5 45	9 20	* 5 23	* 5 23
and every 20 mins. until	6 0	6 0	9 40	5 45	5 45
p.m.	6 15	6 15	and every 20 mins.	6 0	6 0
1 0	6 30	6 30	until	6 15	6 15
1 16	6 38	6 38	p.m.	6 23	6 23
1 24	6 45	6 45	1 0	6 30	6 30
1 32	6 53	6 53	1 8	6 38	6 38
1 40	7 0	7 0	1 16	6 45	6 45
1 48	7 8	and ev. 5 mins. until	1 24	6 53	and every 5 mins. until
1 56	7 12	8 45	1 32	6 57	8 30
2 4	7 15	and every 4 mins. until	1 40	7 0	and ev. 3 & 4 mins. until
2 10	and every 4 mins. until	11 54	1 48	and every 4 mins. until	8 50
and every 5 mins. until	8 27	and ev. 3 mins. until	1 55	8 12	and every 4 mins. until
4 30	and every 3 mins. until	12 38 p.m.	and every 5 mins. until	8 51	11 44
and ev. 4 & 5 mins. until	9 10	and ev. 4 & 5 mins. until	4 5	8 55	and ev. 3 mins. until
5 10	and ev. 5 mins. until	1 29	and every 4 and	12 00	p.m.
and every 5 mins. until	11 50	and ev. 3 & 4 mins. until	5 mins. until	and ev. 3 & 4 mins. until	12 30
10 15	and ev. 3 & 4 mins. until	7 50	4 50	2 40 p.m.	and ev. 3 & 4 mins. until
and ev. 4 & 5 mins. until	p.m.	and every 5 mins. until	and every 5	and every 5 mins. until	7 30
10 45	2 55	9 25	mins. until	4 20	and every 5 mins. until
p.m.	and every 5 mins. until	and ev. 4 & 5 mins. until	10 0	and every 3 mins. until	9 10
	3 55	10 0	and every 4 and	6 00	9 17
	and every 4 mins. until	and every 4 mins. until	5 mins. until	and every 4 and 5 mins. until	and ev. 4 & 5 mins. until
	4 20	11 0	10 30	7 24	9 40
	and every 3 mins. until	p.m.	p.m.	and every 6 mins. until	and every 4 mins. until
	6 03			9 36	10 44
	and every 4 and 5 mins. until			and ev. 4 & 5 mins. until	p.m.
	7 39			10 44	
	and every 6 mins. until			p.m.	
	9 21				
	and ev. 4 & 5 mins. until				
	11 0				
	p.m.				

* Ser. 9 Motorbus

* Ser. 9 Motorbus

Service 71. The route number "71" denotes additional trolley buses on this service running between Paragon Street and Boulevard only.

84.   Wheeler Street Garage was reached by a single set of wires along Wheeler Street itself. Trolleybuses could enter the street from both directions with the majority entering from the direction of Meadowbank Road. Some peak hour workings worked only as far as the garage and displayed "GARAGE" in the via box or on the full pre-war style box. On 12th September 1958 Sunbeam W no. 89 is about to enter Wheeler Street from the city centre, before unloading its remaining passengers who can be seen on the platform. (R. F. Mack)

85.   When service 69 opened in June 1942, trolleybuses terminated by turning via the roundabout at the junction of Anlaby Road and Boothferry Road. Not until 30th March 1947 was the route extended to Meadowbank Road. On a quiet day, Sunbeam W no. 82 passes the location of the original inward stop bound for the city centre.
(Authors' collections)

86.   Another view of the Meadowbank Road terminus shows a 1948 Sunbeam F4 no. 97 leaving for town, whilst the crew of Brush bodied Sunbeam W no. 70 gather for a chat and a smoke. (Authors' collections)

87.   On the last day of service 69 operation, the surviving thirteen Crossley TDD4 trolleybuses were in use. Here no. 41 negotiates the roundabout on its way to the terminus. The date is 3rd February 1962. (M. J. Wells)

HESSLE ROAD

88.   Another royal visit, on 6th November 1960, is thought to be the reason for services 69 and
70 being turned short at Anne Street. Sunbeam W no. 80 has already been dealt with and will use
its normal service 70 wires to set off for Dairycoates. Sunbeam F4 no. 92 is being shunted into
Anne Street and will shortly reverse into Carr Lane to regain the service 69 outward wires.

89. Saturday, 25th October 1958, was the last day, of trolleybus operation along the short Midland Street. From the following day inward journeys on service 70 would be re-routed along Osborne Street and the new Ferensway South extension. The new wires can be seen already in place but unconnected, as yet. The front trolleybus is Sunbeam W no. 83, which is leading a Brush-bodied Sunbeam F4 towards Anlaby Road. (G. M. O'Connell)

90. Crossley TDD4 no. 33 turns into Chariot Street from Paragon Street on the last day of service 70 operation, 28th January 1961. No. 33 will be withdrawn in the late evening. (A. D. Packer)

91.   Service 70 was always the route for the Brush-bodied Sunbeam Ws from inauguration in July 1945 to closure in January 1961. No. 70 is traversing Porter Street on its way to Dairycoates, probably on a Saturday, as there is a wedding car in view. In its later years no. 70 had the curious upper deck arrangement whereby the first half-drop opening window on both sides had been replaced with a sliding window. (Authors' collections)

92.   The eastern part of Hessle Road was narrower than the Dairycoates end, as can be seen in this photograph of Sunbeam W no. 82. The location is near Neptune Street, the first stage point from the city centre, in August 1954. (Authors' collections)

93.   Still in original condition, Sunbeam W no. 78 nears the end of Liverpool Street and prepares to turn left into Hessle Road in order to reach the terminus. This photograph was taken in October 1954 and of all the buildings in view only the Maltby's store still survives, still owned by the family and still a pet shop. (J. Fozard)

94.   Two classes that were also associated with the route throughout the fifties were the majestic F4s and the 1945/6 Sunbeam Ws, of which nos 91 and 79 are shown at Dairycoates. No. 79 was delivered with a destination box and blinds at the rear, but, in this picture the area had been completely panelled over. On some vehicles the aperture was merely painted over. We have not discovered a photograph of the rear box in use on nos 79 to 84. (R. F. Mack)

95.   The Hessle Road route enjoyed a peak frequency of two minutes, which required eighteen trolleybuses. This headway was often interrupted by the level crossings so it was not unusual to see several trolleybuses at the Dairycoates terminus at any one time. Sunbeam W no. 69 is leaving the terminus for the city centre on 8th October 1960. This was the only member of the class to have an area of white between the upper streamlined white line and the destination box. Sunbeam W no. 84 occupies the inward stop and nos 75 and 80 are at last outward stop. (Authors' collections)

96.   The twelve Sunbeam Ws with Brush utility bodywork opened the Dairycoates route in July 1945. As shown here, they were delivered in an allover azure blue livery. No. 68 is the trolleybus at Dairycoates in July 1945. (KHCA)

97. Sunbeam W no. 90 has yet to move to the actual stop, having been drawn up behind another trolleybus. Traffic seems unusually light although there is, inevitably, a queue for the crossing. (Authors' collections)

Service 70. Paragon Street—Dairycoates (Carlton Street) via Hessle Road.

From PARAGON STREET.

Sunday	Monday to Friday		Saturday
a.m.	a.m.	p.m.	a.m.
9 20	* 5 15	6 14	* 5 15
9 40	* 5 30	6 17	* 5 30
10 0	* 5 45	6 20	* 5 45
10 20	* 6 5	and every 3 and	* 6 5
10 40	* 6 20	4 mins. until	* 6 20
11 0	6 45	7 48	6 45
11 15	6 50	and every 4 and	6 50
and every	6 55	5 mins. until	6 55
10 mins. until	7 0	9 54	7 0
p.m.	7 4	and every	7 5
12 5	7 8	3 mins. until	7 10
12 14	7 12	10 40	7 15
12 24	7 15	10 43	and every 3
and every	and every 2 and	10 46	mins. until
6 mins. until	3 mins. until	10 50	11 47
1 00	8 15	10 55	and every 2 and
and every 3 and	and every	11 0 p.m.	3 mins. until
4 mins. until	3 mins. until		5 47
10 45 p.m.	11 44		5 50
	11 47		5 56
	11 49		and every 3 and
	11 52		4 mins. until
	11 55		8 15
	and every 2 and		and every
	3 mins. until		4 & 5 mins. until
	4 26		9 38
	4 27		9 43
	and every		and every 3 and
	2 mins. until		4 mins. until
	6 9		10 40
	6 12		10 43
			11 46
			10 49
			10 52
			10 56
			11 0 p.m.

* Ser. 3 Motorbus

From CARLTON STREET

Sunday	Monday to Friday		Saturday
a.m.	a.m.	p.m.	a.m.
9 0	* 4 58	5 51	* 4 58
9 20	* 5 13	and every 3 and	* 5 13
9 40	* 5 28	4 mins. until	* 5 28
10 0	* 5 43	7 34	* 5 43
10 20	* 5 58	and every 4 and	* 5 58
10 40	* 6 13	5 mins. until	* 6 13
11 0	6 30	9 40	6 30
11 10	6 35	and every 3	6 35
and every	6 40	mins. until	6 40
10 mins. until	6 45	10 32	6 45
p.m.	6 49	10 36	6 50
12 10	6 53	10 40	6 55
and every	6 57	10 45 p.m.	7 0
6 mins. until	7 0		7 3
12 40	and every 2 and		7 6
and every 5	3 mins. until		and every 3
mins. until	8 0		mins. until
1 20	8 3		11 30
and every 3 and	8 6		and every 2 and
4 mins. until	and every		3 mins. until
10 30 p.m.	3 mins. until		p.m.
	11 32		5 30
	11 34		and every
	11 36		3 mins. until
	and every 2 and		6 24
	3 mins. until		6 28
	4 6		and every 3 and
	and every		4 mins. until
	2 mins. until		8 4
	5 48		and every
			4 & 5 mins. until
* Ser. 3 Motorbus			9 24
			9 29
			and every 3 and
			4 mins. until
			10 38
			10 41
			10 45 p.m.

98.   In the last few days of service 70 operation, Leyland TB7 no. 54 has just arrived at Dairycoates and will shortly turn and stand behind Sunbeam W no. 70. The TB7s looked out of place on Hessle Road and were not as comfortable as the F4s. (D. F. Parker)

99.   With the City's registry office in the background, Leyland TB7 no.66 stops at a combined bus and trolleybus stop near the College of Technology in George Street. Behind the AEC Regent III is North Bridge. (Authors' collections)

Service 64. Paragon Square—Ings Road via Holderness Road

From PARAGON SQUARE			From INGS ROAD		
Sunday	Monday to Friday	Saturday	Sunday	Monday to Friday	Saturday
a.m.	a.m.	a.m.	a.m.	a.m.	a.m.
9 20	5 18	5 18	6 58	4 55	4 55
9 40	5 30	5 30	9 00	5 12	5 12
10 00	5 54	5 54	& every 20	5 36	5 36
10 20	6 18	6 18	mins. until	5 53	5 53
10 40	6 30	6 30	11 00	6 00	6 00
11 00	6 42	6 42	& every 10	6 12	6 12
11 20	6 50	6 48	mins. until	6 24	6 24
& every 10	& every 5	6 54	p.m.	6 30	6 30
mins. until	mins. until	7 00	1 00	& every 5	6 36
p.m.	8 10	& every 5	1 07	mins. until	6 42
1 00	8 18	mins. until	1 15	8 00	6 45
1 09	8 45	8 45	1 22	8 03	& every 5
1 20	8 55	8 55	1 30	& every 6	mins. until
1 27	9 04	& every 5	& every 5	mins. until	8 50
1 35	& every 3	& every 8	mins. until	8 45	8 54
1 42	mins. until	mins. until	9 25	& every 5	9 00
1 50	9 05	11 50	& every 8	mins. until	& every 8
& every 5	& every 5	& every 6	mins. until	p.m.	mins. until
mins. until	p.m.	mins. until	10 21	1 00	11 24
9 10	1 20	12 32	10 26 p.m.	& every 4	11 28
9 20	& every 4	mins. until		mins. until	& every 6
9 25	mins. until	& every 3 or		2 40	mins. until
9 35	3 00	4 mins. until		& every 5	p.m.
9 44	& every 5	4 31		mins. until	12 50
9 52	mins. until	& every 6		4 15	& every 3 or
10 06	4 15	mins. until		& every 6	4 mins. until
10 08	& every 6	5 49		4 mins. until	4 45
& every 4	mins. until	& every 3		4 45	& every 6
mins. until	5 33	mins. until		6 47	mins. until
10 40	& every 3	7 07		& every 4	6 05
10 45 p.m.	mins. until	& every 6		mins. until	& every 3
	5 57	mins. until		7 35	mins. until
	6 05	7 37		& every 5	7 21
	6 13	7 42		mins. until	& every
	6 21	& every 3		10 10	5 or 6
	6 29	mins. until		10 14	mins. until
	& every 4	8 20		10 20	10 39
	mins. until	& every 5 or		10 27	10 42 p.m.
	7 25	6 mins. until		10 36	
	& every 5	10 21		10 42 p.m.	
	mins. until	& every 3			
	10 00	mins. until			
	& every 4	11 00 p.m.			
	mins. until				
	11 00 p.m.				

: Ser. 56 Motorbus
• Ser. 58 Motorbus

Service 68. Paragon Square—East Park via Holderness Rd.
Consolidated time-table of Services 64 and 68.

From PARAGON SQUARE			From EAST PARK		
Sunday	Monday to Friday	Saturday	Sunday	Monday to Friday	Saturday
a.m.	a.m.	a.m.	a.m.	a.m.	a.m.
9 20	5 18	5 18	6 58	4 58	4 58
9 40	5 30	5 30	9 03	5 15	5 15
10 00	5 54	5 54	9 23	5 39	5 39
10 20	6 18	6 18	9 43	5 56	5 56
10 40	6 30	6 30	10 03	6 03	6 03
11 00	6 42	6 42	10 23	6 15	6 12
11 20	6 50	6 48	10 43	6 27	6 27
& every 10	& every 5	6 54	11 03	6 33	6 33
mins. until	mins. until	7 00	& every 10	& every 5	6 39
p.m.	8 15	& every 5	mins. until	mins. until	6 45
1 00		mins. until	p.m.	8 03	& every 5
1 09	& every 3	9 00	1 03	& every 3	mins. until
1 20	mins. until	& every 3 &	1 10	mins. until	8 50
1 27	9 05	4 mins. until	1 18	8 48	& every 3
1 35	& every 5	p.m.	1 25	& every 5	& 4 mins.
1 42	mins. until	8 20	1 33	mins. until	until
1 50	p.m.	& every 5	& every 5	p.m.	p.m.
& every 5	1 20	mins. until	mins. until	1 03	8 03
mins. until	& every 4	9 30	9 28	& every 4	& every 5
9 40	mins. until	& every 3	& every 4	mins. until	mins. until
& every 4	3 00	& every 4	mins. until	2 43	9 18
mins. until	& every 5	mins. until	mins. until	& every 5	& every 3
10 40	mins. until	11 00 p.m.	10 28 p.m.	mins. until	mins. until
10 45 p.m.	4 10			3 48	10 45 p.m.
	& every 3			& every 3	
	mins. until			mins. until	
	5 57			5 49	
	& every 4			& every 4	
	mins. until			mins. until	
	7 25			7 38	
	& every 5			& every 5	
	mins. until			mins. until	
	10 00			9 43	
	& every 4			& every 4	
	mins. until			mins. until	
	11 00 p.m.			10 45 p.m.	

: Ser. 56 Motorbus
• Ser. 58 Motorbus

100. From July 1952, alternate trolleybuses on the Holderness Road were cut back to East Park during the quieter off-peak periods as service 68 in order to save 60,000 miles and £3,000 annually. The two services were interworked and blinds were changed in Savile Street before vehicles reached the Jameson Street terminus. Having assisted with the positioning of no. 64's blind, the conductor, who is wearing his lighter summer jacket, is returning to the platform. (R. F. Mack)

Service 69. Paragon Street—Meadowbank Road
via Anlaby Road.

From PARAGON STREET			From MEADOWBANK ROAD		
Sunday	Monday to Friday	Saturday	Sunday	Monday to Friday	Saturday
a.m.	a.m.	a.m.	a.m.	a.m.	a m.
9 20	5 15	5 15	9 0	5 0	5 0
9 40	* 5 45	* 5 45	9 20	* 5 23	* 5 23
and every 20 mins. until	6 0	6 0	9 40	5 45	5 45
p.m.	6 15	6 15	and every 20 mins.	6 0	6 0
1 0	6 30	6 30	until	6 15	6 15
1 16	6 38	6 38	p.m.	6 23	6 23
1 24	6 45	6 45	1 0	6 30	6 30
1 32	6 53	6 53	1 8	6 38	6 38
1 40	7 0	7 0	1 16	6 45	6 45
1 48	7 8	and ev. 5 mins. until	1 24	6 53	and every 5 mins. until
1 56	7 12	8 45	1 32	6 57	8 30
2 4	7 15	and every 4 mins. until	1 40	7 0	and ev. 3 & 4 mins. until
2 10	and every 4 mins. until	11 54	1 48	and every 4 mins. until	8 50
and every 5 mins. until	8 27	and ev. 3 mins. until	1 55	8 12	and every 4 mins. until
4 30	and every 3 mins. until	12 38 p.m.	and every 5 mins. until	and every 3 mins. until	11 44
and ev. 4 & 5 mins. until	9 10	and ev. 4 & 5 mins. until	4 5	8 51	and ev. 3 mins. until
5 10	and every 5 mins. until	1 29	and every 4 and	8 55	p.m.
and ev. 5 mins. until	11 50	and ev. 3 & 4 mins. until	5 mins. until	and every 5 mins. until	12 30
10 15	and ev. 3 & 4 mins. until	7 50	4 50	12 00	and ev. 3 & 4 mins. until
and ev. 4 & 5 mins. until	p.m.	and every 5 mins. until	and every 5	and ev. 3 & 4 mins. until	7 30
10 45	2 55	9 25	mins. until	2 40 p.m.	and every 5 mins. until
p.m.	and every 5 mins. until	and ev. 4 & 5 mins. until	10 00	and every 5 mins. until	9 10
	3 55	10 0	and every 4 and	4 20	9 17
	and every 4 mins. until	and every 4 mins. until	5 mins. until	and every 3 mins. until	and ev. 4 & 5 mins. until
	4 20	11 0	10 30	6 00	9 40
	and every 3 mins. until	p.m.	p.m.	7 24	and every 4 mins. until
	6 03			and every 4 and 5 mins. until	10 44
	and every 4 and 5 mins. until			9 36	p.m.
	7 39			and ev. 4 & 5 mins. until	
	and every 6 mins. until			10 44	
	9 21		* Ser. 9 Motorbus	p.m.	
* Ser. 9 Motorbus	and ev. 4 & 5 mins. until				
	11 0				
	p.m.				

Service 71. The route number "71" denotes additional trolley buses on this service running between Paragon Street and Boulevard only.

101. Two of the imposing eight feet wide Sunbeam F4s (nos 98 and 100) are seen opposite the
Co-op in Jameson Street. This section of overhead formed part of the original terminal loop for
the Holderness Road trolleybuses. The loop was retained after the 1940 extension to the railway
station, but was little used until March 1959, when this section was incorporated into the revised
routeing. (R. F. Mack)

102. This photograph provides a good view of the rear of the East Lancashire bodywork on Leyland TB7s nos 47 to 66. The painted over rear destination screen can be seen as well as the red triangle in the centre of the lower deck window, which was used to inform following drivers that no. 59 is a trolleybus. Across the road work is in progress on the diversion of services 64 and 68. No. 59 has just vacated the terminus outside Hammonds in Jameson Street and is bound for Ings Road.(R. F. Mack)

103. Leyland TB7 no. 48 unloads its last passengers outside the Imperial Hotel in Paragon Street shortly after services 64/8 were re-routed in March 1959. No 48 was purchased for service 64 in 1939, but entered service on the northern routes on 31st August 1939 from Cottingham Road. It was transferred to Holderness Road, when the route finally opened in February 1940. (Authors' collections)

104. The 1947 Sunbeam Ws carried Roe H60R bodies of classical lines. They were initially allocated to Cottingham Road Garage but throughout the late fifties they were to be found on services 69 and 70. They resembled the F4s (nos 91 - 100) but were to the narrower width of 7' 6". The difference in width can be seen in this photograph, on 7th April 1961, showing nos 85 and 94 in South Street (Authors' collections).

FINALE

105. Saturday, 31st October 1964, was the last day of trolleybus operation in Hull. It was a wet and foggy day, and the elements combined to thwart most photographers. Some were fortunate, so that we are able to view "Coronation" no. 101 just before the final service 63 departure in Chapel Street, although the bus stop already carried the new motorbus service details. The duplicate trolleybus, no. 116, has just departed and Motorman Gill Sewell and conductor Bob Leonard will have the distinction of crewing Hull's last trolleybus. There was no official acknowledgement of the historic event and Hull's trolleybuses would quietly fade away. (Authors' collections)

GARAGES AND WORKSHOPS

106. The Liverpool Street complex included the main workshops, paintshop and the trolleybus garage (formerly a tram depot) for service 70. A new entrance had to be created for trolleybuses in the side of the road towards the rear of the building at the top left hand corner of the photograph. Trolleybuses left the garage through the original doorway immediately behind the photographer. Sunbeam W no. 84 was caught in the running shed on 16th May 1953. In addition to the eighteen trolleybuses allocated to service 70, other trolleybuses could often be seen awaiting works attention or immediately after a repaint. (J. Fozard)

107. The paintshop was situated at the rear of the trolleybus garage where, on 26th May 1955, Leyland TB7 no.58 was receiving the final touches to its repaint before being sent back to Holderness Road. No. 58 has received the narrower side white band below the upper deck windows, which all trolleybuses were given from the mid-fifties. (R. F. Mack)

Service 70. Paragon Street—Dairycoates (Carlton Street) via Hessle Road.

From PARAGON STREET.

Sunday
a.m.
9 20
9 40
10 0
10 20
10 40
11 0
11 15
and every
10 mins. until
p.m.
12 5
12 14
12 24
and every
6 mins. until
1 00
and every 3 and
4 mins. until
10 45 p.m.

Monday to Friday

a.m.
* 5 15
* 5 30
* 5 45
* 6 5
* 6 20
6 45
6 50
6 55
7 0
7 4
7 8
7 12
7 15
and every 2 and
3 mins. until
8 15
and every
3 mins. until
11 44
11 47
11 49
11 52
11 55
and every 2 and
3 mins. until
4 26
4 27
and every
2 mins. until
6 9
6 12

p.m.
6 14
6 17
6 20
and every 3 and
4 mins. until
7 48
and every 4 and
5 mins. until
9 54
and every
3 mins. until
10 40
10 43
10 46
10 50
10 55
11 0 p.m.

Saturday
a.m.
* 5 15
* 5 30
* 5 45
* 6 5
* 6 20
6 45
6 50
6 55
7 0
7 5
7 10
7 15
and every 3
mins. until
11 47
and every 2 and
3 mins. until
5 47
5 50
5 53
5 56
and every 3 and
4 mins. until
8 15
and every
4 & 5 mins. until
9 38
9 43
and every 3 and
4 mins. until
10 40
10 43
10 46
10 49
10 52
10 56
11 0 p.m.

* Ser. 3 Motorbus

From CARLTON STREET

Sunday
a.m.
9 0
9 20
9 40
10 0
10 20
10 40
11 0
11 10
and every
10 mins. until
p.m.
12 10
and every
6 mins. until
12 40
and every 5
mins. until
1 20
and every 3 and
4 mins until
10 30 p.m.

* Ser. 3 Motorbus

Monday to Friday

a.m.
* 4 58
* 5 13
* 5 28
* 5 43
* 5 58
* 6 13
6 30
6 35
6 40
6 45
6 49
6 53
6 57
7 0
and every 2 and
3 mins until
8 0
8 3
8 6
and every
3 mins. until
11 32
11 34
11 36
and every 2 and
3 mins. until
4 6
and every
2 mins. until
5 48

p.m.
5 51
and every 3 and
4 mins. until
7 34
and every 4 and
5 mins. until
9 40
and every 3
mins. until
10 32
10 36
10 40
10 45 p.m.

Saturday
a.m.
* 4 58
* 5 13
* 5 28
* 5 43
* 5 58
* 6 13
6 30
6 35
6 40
6 45
6 50
6 55
7 0
7 3
7 6
and every 3
mins. until
11 30
and every 2 and
3 mins. until
p.m.
5 30
and every
3 mins. until
6 24
6 28
and every 3
mins. until
8 4
and every
4 & 5 mins. until
9 24
9 29
and every 3 and
4 mins. until
10 38
10 41
10 45 p.m.

108. A previous photograph, no.83 showed the narrowness of the exit from Wheeler Street Garage. The rear was very spacious as can be seen in this view which shows Sunbeams 92 and 87 resting between duties. (R. F. Mack)

109. Les Storry's son faces the camera outside Holderness Road garage on what is probably a Sunday morning. In addition to the home resident Leyland TB7s, Crossley no. 33 is also in residence, but will soon leave to begin its daily work. (Authors' collections)

110. Trolleybuses from Cottingham Road are being prepared to work dance specials, as other trolleybuses come home after their day's work. No. 108 is displaying the number 13, which indicates that it will work along Beverley Road from King Edward Street. Extras on Newland Avenue displayed number 12. Trolleybuses occupied the area seen, whilst motorbuses and overhead line vehicles were stabled to the left. (Authors' collections)

111. An important part of any garage's facilities was the bus washing machine. Having just completed its tour of duty on service 61, Crossley TDD4 no. 44 is driven through the Cottingham Road washer before being parked on the other side of the garage. (R. F. Mack)

ROLLING STOCK

Nos 1 - 26 (CRH 925-950) built 1937, withdrawn 1952-55.

112. The Weymann H54R bodies fitted to Leyland TB4 chassis were equipped with concealed trolley gantries that resulted in a simple, clean and neat design. Some crews referred to them as "Little Leylands" to distinguish them from the later TB7s even though they had practically the same dimensions! No.15 is pictured in the original livery. (Hull Daily Mail)

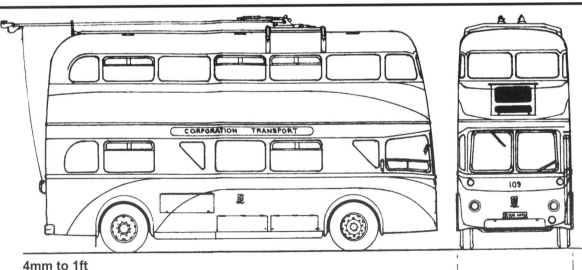

4mm to 1ft

8'-0"

Nos 27 - 46 (ERH 27-46) built 1938, withdrawn 1954-1962.

113. The twenty Crossley TDD4s proved to be an excellent investment with an average working life of twenty-three years. Originally purchased for service 63, which they worked exclusively until wartime requirements decreed otherwise, they were closely associated with service 62 throughout the 1950s. No. 38, newly repainted, shows off its Cravens bodywork outside Cottingham Road garage. (J. Fozard)

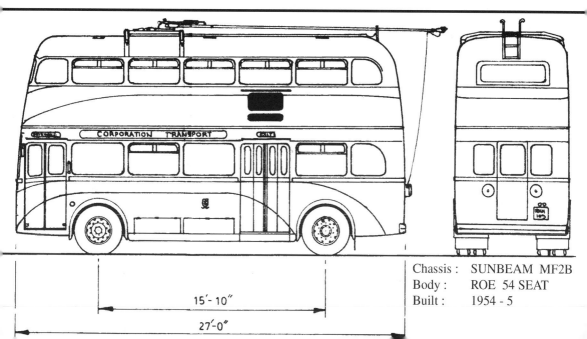

15'- 10"

27'-0"

Chassis :	SUNBEAM MF2B
Body :	ROE 54 SEAT
Built :	1954 - 5

Nos 47 - 66 (FRH 547-566) built 1939, withdrawn 1957-61.

114. These Leyland TB7 had East Lancashire bodywork that resembled those built by Cravens in 1938. Nos 50 and 63 rest in the yard at the rear of Holderness Road Garage, before the entry and exit arrangements were reversed. Behind no. 50 can be seen the scoreboard at the adjoining Craven Park ground that was the home of Hull Kingston Rovers rugby club and was also the local greyhound track. Crews were able to watch games from the upper deck of those strategically placed vehicles! The date was 19th October 1952. (Authors' collections)

Nos 67 - 78 (GRH 287 - 298) built 1945, withdrawn 1962-3.

115. These trolleybuses were used to replace the city's last trams on 1st July 1945. They were Sunbeam Ws with Brush UH56R bodies and were delivered in an allover azure blue livery, but were soon repainted into the standard colours. In June 1946, no. 72 was posed for official photographs outside the front of the City Hall. The angular lines of the bodywork are clearly shown and the first version of the "CORPORATION TRANSPORT" legend can also be seen. (KHCA)

Nos 79 - 84 (GRH 355-360) built 1945, withdrawn 1962-3.

116. Nos 79 to 84 were delivered in late 1945 and were painted in an allover navy blue livery. They were Sunbeam Ws and carried Roe H56R bodies to a more relaxed utility design, that contained several classical Roe features such as the raised waist rail. No. 80 is seen after reversing into Malm Street, and carries the standard number and via point display at the front. Over the platform it is fitted with a wartime large service number blind. Some of these survived into the mid-fifties, as did some of the pre-war white blinds. Indeed no. 80 was photographed with such a blind in June 1955. No. 83 was withdrawn in September 1963, but survived in a Bingley scrapyard until 1983, when the City Museum staff considered it too far gone to be worth saving. (R. F. Mack)

Nos 85 - 90 (HAT 85 - 90) built 1947, withdrawn 1963.

117. These six Sunbeams carried H60R bodywork that marked a return to the classical Roe shape and the installation on a nearside cab door. They were the first trolleybuses to carry the new standard destination arrangement of two large service numbers and a narrow rectangular slot to display the name of the major road along which it travelled. No. 95 is pictured at Meadowbank Road. (Authors' collections)

Nos 91 - 100 (HRH 91-100) built 1948, withdrawn 1963.

118.   These Sunbeam F4s were fitted with Roe H60R eight feet wide bodies of majestic proportions and were well regarded by management, staff and passengers alike. All entered service on 1st June 1948 on service 69 from Wheeler Street garage. No 97 was specially posed at Chariot Street, sometime in May 1948, before being licensed. Withdrawal took place on the conversion of service 62 in November 1963 after a life of only fifteen years. (KHCA)

Nos 101 - 116 (NRH 101, RKH 102 - 116) built 1952-5, withdrawn 1964.

IF ONLY!

Nos 1 - 10 for delivery late 1959.

119. The "Coronations " had Sunbeam MF2B chassis with Roe H54D bodies of a pleasing nature. The prototype, no. 101, entered service in January 1953 but is seen here shortly before that date at Cottingham Road Garage. It lacks the entrance sign in the forward side window but is otherwise ready for service.
(Authors' collections)

120. In December 1958 the General Manager, Mr Pulfrey, was authorised to purchase ten thirty-five feet long Sunbeam single deck trolleybuses (to be numbered 1 to 10) to be fitted with Roe bodies for operation on a pay as you enter basis on services 61/5. Events leading to the decision to abandon trolleybus operation overtook the order, which was never confirmed. This model was constructed by the late Mr Geoff O'Connell (Traffic Officer) and shows how the vehicles may have looked. Staff at the city's Street Life Museum made the model specially available for photography..
(J. S. Wells)

Middleton Press

Easebourne Lane, Midhurst, W Sussex. GU29 9AZ Tel: 01730 813169 Fax: 01730 812601
Email: sales@middletonpress.co.uk   www.middletonpress.co.uk
If books are not available from your local transport stockist, order direct post free UK.

BRANCH LINES
Branch Line to Allhallows
Branch Line to Alton
Branch Lines around Ascot
Branch Line to Ashburton
Branch Lines around Bodmin
Branch Line to Bude
Branch Lines around Canterbury
Branch Lines around Chard & Yeovil
Branch Line to Cheddar
Branch Lines around Cromer
Branch Line to the Derwent Valley
Branch Lines to East Grinstead
Branch Lines of East London
Branch Lines to Effingham Junction
Branch Lines around Exmouth
Branch Lines to Falmouth, Helston & St. Ives
Branch Line to Fairford
Branch Lines to Felixstow & Aldeburgh
Branch Lines around Gosport
Branch Line to Hayling
Branch Lines to Henley, Windsor & Marlow
Branch Line to Hawkhurst
Branch Line to Horsham
Branch Lines around Huntingdon
Branch Line to Ilfracombe
Branch Line to Kingsbridge
Branch Line to Kingswear
Branch Line to Lambourn
Branch Lines to Launceston & Princetown
Branch Lines to Longmoor
Branch Line to Looe
Branch Line to Lyme Regis
Branch Line to Lynton
Branch Lines around March
Branch Lines around Midhurst
Branch Line to Minehead
Branch Line to Moretonhampstead
Branch Lines to Newport (IOW)
Branch Lines to Newquay
Branch Lines around North Woolwich
Branch Line to Padstow
Branch Lines to Princes Risborough
Branch Lines to Seaton and Sidmouth
Branch Lines around Sheerness
Branch Line to Shrewsbury
Branch Line to Tenterden
Branch Lines around Tiverton
Branch Lines to Torrington
Branch Lines to Tunbridge Wells
Branch Line to Upwell
Branch Line to Wantage (The Wantage Tramway)
Branch Lines of West London
Branch Lines of West Wiltshire
Branch Lines around Weymouth
Branch Lines around Wimborne
Branch Lines around Wisbech

NARROW GAUGE
Austrian Narrow Gauge
Branch Line to Lynton
Branch Lines around Portmadoc 1923-46
Branch Lines around Porthmadog 1954-94
Branch Line to Southwold
Douglas to Port Erin
Douglas to Peel
Kent Narrow Gauge
Northern France Narrow Gauge
Romneyrail
Southern France Narrow Gauge
Sussex Narrow Gauge
Surrey Narrow Gauge

Swiss Narrow Gauge
Two-Foot Gauge Survivors
Vivarais Narrow Gauge

SOUTH COAST RAILWAYS
Ashford to Dover
Bournemouth to Weymouth
Brighton to Worthing
Dover to Ramsgate
Eastbourne to Hastings
Hastings to Ashford
Portsmouth to Southampton
Ryde to Ventnor
Southampton to Bournemouth

SOUTHERN MAIN LINES
Basingstoke to Salisbury
Crawley to Littlehampton
Dartford to Sittingbourne
East Croydon to Three Bridges
Epsom to Horsham
Exeter to Barnstaple
Exeter to Tavistock
London Bridge to East Croydon
Orpington to Tonbridge
Tonbridge to Hastings
Salisbury to Yeovil
Sittingbourne to Ramsgate
Swanley to Ashford
Tavistock to Plymouth
Three Bridges to Brighton
Victoria to Bromley South
Victoria to East Croydon
Waterloo to Windsor
Waterloo to Woking
Woking to Portsmouth
Woking to Southampton
Yeovil to Exeter

EASTERN MAIN LINES
Barking to Southend
Ely to Kings Lynn
Ely to Norwich
Fenchurch Street to Barking
Hitchin to Peterborough
Ilford to Shenfield
Ipswich to Saxmundham
Liverpool Street to Ilford
Saxmundham to Yarmouth
Tilbury Loop

WESTERN MAIN LINES
Bristol to Taunton
Didcot to Banbury
Didcot to Swindon
Ealing to Slough
Exeter to Newton Abbot
Moreton-in-Marsh to Worcester
Newton Abbot to Plymouth
Newbury to Westbury
Oxford to Moreton-in-Marsh
Paddington to Ealing
Paddington to Princes Risborough
Plymouth to St. Austell
Princes Risborough to Banbury
Reading to Didcot
Slough to Newbury
St. Austell to Penzance
Swindon to Bristol
Taunton to Exeter
Westbury to Taunton

MIDLAND MAIN LINES
St. Albans to Bedford
Euston to Harrow & Wealdstone
Harrow to Watford
St. Pancras to St. Albans

COUNTRY RAILWAY ROUTES
Abergavenny to Merthyr
Andover to Southampton
Bath to Evercreech Junction
Bath Green Park to Bristol
Bournemouth to Evercreech Junction
Brecon to Newport
Burnham to Evercreech Junction
Cheltenham to Andover
Croydon to East Grinstead
Didcot to Winchester
East Kent Light Railway
Frome to Bristol
Guildford to Redhill
Reading to Basingstoke
Reading to Guildford
Redhill to Ashford
Salisbury to Westbury
Stratford upon Avon to Cheltenham
Strood to Paddock Wood
Taunton to Barnstaple
Wenford Bridge to Fowey
Westbury to Bath
Woking to Alton
Yeovil to Dorchester

GREAT RAILWAY ERAS
Ashford from Steam to Eurostar
Clapham Junction 50 years of change
Festiniog in the Fifties
Festiniog in the Sixties
Festiniog 50 years of enterprise
Isle of Wight Lines 50 years of change
Railways to Victory 1944-46
Return to Blaenau 1970-82
SECR Centenary album
Talyllyn 50 years of change
Wareham to Swanage 50 years of change
Yeovil 50 years of change

LONDON SUBURBAN RAILWAYS
Caterham and Tattenham Corner
Charing Cross to Dartford
Clapham Jn. to Beckenham Jn.
Crystal Palace (HL) & Catford Loop
East London Line
Finsbury Park to Alexandra Palace
Holborn Viaduct to Lewisham
Kingston and Hounslow Loops
Lewisham to Dartford
Liverpool Street to Chingford
London Bridge to Addiscombe
Mitcham Junction Lines
North London Line
South London Line
West Croydon to Epsom
West London Line
Willesden Junction to Richmond
Wimbledon to Beckenham
Wimbledon to Epsom

STEAMING THROUGH
Steaming through Cornwall
Steaming through the Isle of Wight
Steaming through Kent
Steaming through West Hants

TRAMWAY CLASSICS
Aldgate & Stepney Tramways
Barnet & Finchley Tramways
Bath Tramways
Brighton's Tramways
Bristol's Tramways
Burton & Ashby Tramways
Camberwell & W.Norwood Tramways
Clapham & Streatham Tramways
Croydon's Tramways
Dover's Tramways
East Ham & West Ham Tramways
Edgware and Willesden Tramways
Eltham & Woolwich Tramways
Embankment & Waterloo Tramways
Exeter & Taunton Tramways
Fulwell - Home to Trams, Trolleys and Buses
Great Yarmouth Tramways
Greenwich & Dartford Tramways
Hammersmith & Hounslow Tramways
Hampstead & Highgate Tramways
Hastings Tramways
Holborn & Finsbury Tramways
Ilford & Barking Tramways
Kingston & Wimbledon Tramways
Lewisham & Catford Tramways
Liverpool Tramways 1. Eastern Routes
Liverpool Tramways 2. Southern Routes
Liverpool Tramways 3. Northern Routes
Maidstone & Chatham Tramways
Margate to Ramsgate
North Kent Tramways
Norwich Tramways
Reading Tramways
Seaton & Eastbourne Tramways
Shepherds Bush & Uxbridge Tramways
Southend-on-sea Tramways
South London Line Tramways 1903-33
Southwark & Deptford Tramways
Stamford Hill Tramways
Twickenham & Kingston Tramways
Victoria & Lambeth Tramways
Waltham Cross & Edmonton Tramways
Walthamstow & Leyton Tramways
Wandsworth & Battersea Tramways

TROLLEYBUS CLASSICS
Bradford Trolleybuses
Croydon Trolleybuses
Derby Trolleybuses
Hastings Trolleybuses
Huddersfield Trolleybuses
Hull Trolleybuses
Maidstone Trolleybuses
Portsmouth Trolleybuses
Reading Trolleybuses

WATERWAY & SHIPPING
Kent and East Sussex Waterways
London to Portsmouth Waterway
Sussex Shipping - Sail, Steam & Motor
West Sussex Waterways

MILITARY BOOKS
Battle over Portsmouth
Battle over Sussex 1940
Blitz over Sussex 1941-42
Bombers over Sussex 1943-45
Bognor at War
Military Defence of West Sussex
Military Signals from the South Coast
Secret Sussex Resistance
Surrey Home Guard

OTHER RAILWAY BOOKS
Index to all Middleton Press stations
Industrial Railways of the South-East
South Eastern & Chatham Railways
London Chatham & Dover Railway
London Termini - Past and Proposed
War on the Line (SR 1939-45)